D0492794

Mission Praise

Compiled by

Roland Fudge, Peter Horrobin and Greg Leavers

MUSIC EDITION

Marshall Morgan & Scott

Marshall Morgan & Scott
3 Beggarwood Lane, Basingstoke, Hants, UK

Compilation copyright © Mission England 1983

First published by Marshall Morgan & Scott 1983

Reprinted
Impression number
86 87 88 89: 10 9 8

ISBN: 0 551 01092 4

Printed in Great Britain at The Bath Press, Avon

Foreword

Music unites or divides people at a deep level of their personalities. This is seen in the generation gaps in musical tastes in the secular world and the different music you hear in the various denominations or even groups within the same denomination.

In a time of mission and evangelism, it is vital that the power of music to unite Christians is harnessed. This does not come easily because we all like what we like in music. We need to become familiar with the songs that other Christians sing and encourage them to enjoy what we enjoy.

This book was originally compiled to enable the uniting power of music to operate during and after Mission England. I commend it to all churches and individuals who would like to share in the work of evangelism.

May it awaken memories, surface a sense of need, convey the story of Jesus, open hearts, help people to express personal faith in him and aid Christian growth.

Tom Houston

The Story of this Book

The idea for *Mission England Praise* was born out of need. In the early days of *Mission England*, Christians from various denominations began to meet together to praise God and pray for the work in hand. The hymnbooks available were frequently unfamiliar territory to those present and whilst some of the traditional hymns were usually included it always seemed as though key ones were missing! And only rarely could any of the more recent praise and worship songs be made available for use without breaking the copyright laws!

In February 1983 work began, therefore, to overcome this problem and in November of that year *Mission England Praise* was publicly launched in a series of meetings across the nation. In the intervening period Christians working in areas outside the influence of *Mission England* became aware of the compilation and appreciated its wider potential for both mission use and as a practical supplement to the traditional hymnbook.

The publishers produced, therefore, a *Mission Praise* version, the contents being identical in every other respect to *Mission England Praise*. Such has been the demand for both versions that the publishers have found it hard to keep the book constantly in print – there are now well over 1 million copies of the *Music* and *Words* editions in circulation. There are also special versions for use in South Africa and Australia (known there as *Living Praise*) and for the Crusaders Union (known as *Crusader Praise*).

We are thankful to God that *Mission Praise* has been used so extensively and trust that it will continue to meet a need in the years ahead as Christians share together in the continuing Mission of the Church.

Introduction

This book has been compiled for a purpose: to unite Christians of all denominations in praise and worship as they work together in evangelism. We anticipate, however, that many churches and fellowships will also find this compilation meets their need for a suitable supplement to their usual hymnbook.

We recognise that every user will know additional hymns and songs which they feel should have been included. To satisfy everyone, however, the book would have been of totally uneconomic proportions and we therefore apologise now if some of your favourites have had to be omitted!

Compiling a volume such as this could not have been achieved without the help of many people. Our grateful thanks go to each and everyone. Whilst it would be impractical to try and mention them all by name, special thanks must be expressed to Noel Tredinnick (Director of Music at All Souls, Langham Place), Stanley Grant and Jim Girling (of the publishers) and all those associated with Mission England who so willingly offered their advice and suggestions following the circulation of our original selection of hymns and songs.

We have sought to represent in the contents the many different strands of musical tradition found in today's Christian music, whilst at the same time to include a substantial number of traditional hymns which will be familiar territory, both to regular churchgoers and those for whom singing hymns is only an occasional experience! The arrangement of the book is largely alphabetical – the few exceptions being introduced by the publishers as a necessary economy in laying out the pages of the music edition.

Finally we ask all who use this book to echo our prayer that as people sing from its pages, Christians will be drawn closer to their Lord, and those who have not committed their lives to Jesus Christ may recognise their need of a Saviour and seek Him who died that they may live.

Peter Horrobin

Music and Worship

This book is a declaration of Christian unity. Nevertheless it has been compiled in the full knowledge that all who look into it will initially find some items acceptable and others unacceptable, because our humanity makes us limited in our tastes! Our sense of security in worship too often depends on the use of that which is familiar, or which we would personally choose, but the resulting disagreements, though frequently stubborn, are often reminiscent of the party strife in Gulliver's Travels over whether an egg should be eaten from the big end or the little end!

There is a great joy in purposefully crossing those dividing walls which have caused us to mistrust the naivety of the 'low-brow', the sophistication of the academically respectable, the emotional insistence of the often repeated chorus or the hymn that triggers subjective memories of arid school assemblies. Whatever our predilections, and in no way seeking to negate our individual personalities, let us take pleasure in being the Body of Christ with all its varied limbs and organs, worshiping God together with the full range of mind, emotions, senses and will, under the leading of the Holy Spirit who gives us the freedom to shake off our little securities of 'style' and find our real security in God above.

For those exploring the unfamiliar the many simple piano arrangements should serve as an introduction to the style of each item. They can be used as they are, but for accompanying large numbers of people, filling out will probably be necessary, according to the judgement and ability of the player. Additional instruments can be used as appropriate and available. Often the base line of the harmony will need reinforcing by octave doubling or an additional bass instrument. Organists could play the bass line of the guitar chords on the pedals, especially when the written-out left hand part is more pianistic than organ-like.

The musicians should always give a clear lead to the people, so extreme elaboration should be avoided unless the singing is very secure, and the words should serve as a guide to the nature of any elaboration.

Never forget the joyfulness of the Christian Gospel, especially in the slower and quieter songs, which should never sound weary or funereal, but should be sung with an inner knowledge that God is looking at us with love because we are in Christ Jesus. Choirs and other worship leaders should regularly pray that this love will show in their voices and faces.

Be open to the use of sequences of songs within an unbroken flow of praise and worship; the shorter choruses are often most effectively used this way and can be repeated several times to encourage a sense of remaining in meditation, or emphasising an important thought. Sometimes the worship will naturally become silent for a while.

It is good to plan prayerfully and it is good to be flexible during the times of worship, so that these times of meeting in the presence of the Living God can be a real sharing of the Living Water which flows to bring about the fulfilment of God's purposes.

Roland Fudge

Notes for Guitarists

The original concept for this book allowed for many considerations. Of these, the addition of guitar chords to the music for all the hymns and songs was high on the list. For in a growing number of church and fellowship situations the guitar is the primary instrument for leading worship. But this growth appears to have been accompanied by a certain amount of complacency amongst some guitarists who try to get by with using as few chords as possible!

We do appreciate, however, that the experience and ability of guitarists varies considerably and we have, therefore, attempted to make the arrangements as simple as possible without destroying the richness of the music. We suggest that if your chord knowledge is currently very limited that it would be well worthwhile learning a few more chords (e.g. F# m, C# m, Bm, Gm, B♭ and diminished chords), for you would then be able to play nearly all the hymns and songs we have included. At the back of the book you will find an easy-to-use chord chart which will enable you to learn all the chords you will need.

To enable relatively simple chords to be regularly used we have often included two sets of chords, so that with the use of a capo, as directed at the top of the music, the guitarist can follow the set of easier bracketed chords e.g. E♭ (D). Where a chord is written, e.g. $\frac{A}{C\#}$ the top letter is the chord, and the bottom letter is the bass note. If you know how to play the chord with the appropriate bass note, do so, if not just play the chord (the top letter). Bass guitarists should follow the chords, or bass note where it is given beneath the chord.

We want guitarists to enjoy their playing, but we also want to encourage those with limited ability to learn new chords and techniques. Here are a few practical tips:

1. Practice strumming so that you learn what types of rhythm suit particular sorts of hymn. If you have a steel strung guitar, get used to using a plectrum
2. Be confident when you lead. Practice does make an enormous difference!! You will find that people will sing confidently if you play confidently.
3. Learn the chords well so that you don't have to stop half way through a song to look one up in the chord chart.
4. Make sure your guitar is in tune, (i) with itself, and (ii) with any other instrument you're playing along with.
5. Make sure you and any other instrument player know what key you are going to play a particular song in.
6. Lastly, but most importantly, pray about your music. Don't just treat it as a hobby but see it as a ministry through which the Lord can draw people's attention to Himself.

Greg Leavers

1 Abba Father

D. Bilbrough *arr.* R. Fudge

Thoughtfully

Ab - ba Fa - ther, let me be Yours and Yours a-lone. May my will for - e - ver be Ev - er more Your own. Ne - ver let my heart grow cold. Ne - ver let me go, Ab - ba Father let me be Yours and Yours a - lone.

2 Abide with me

EVENTIDE 10 10 10 10

W.H. Monk

1 Abide with me; fast falls the eventide;
  The darkness deepens; Lord, with me abide
  When other helpers fail, and comforts flee,
  Help of the helpless, O abide with me.

2 Swift to its close ebbs out life's little day;
  Earth's joys grow dim, its glories pass away;
  Change and decay in all around I see:
  O Thou who changest not, abide with me!

3 I need Thy presence every passing hour;
  What but Thy grace can foil the tempter's power?
  Who like Thyself my guide and stay can be?
  Through cloud and sunshine, O abide with me.

4 I fear no foe, with Thee at hand to bless;
  Ills have no weight, and tears no bitterness;
  Where is death's sting? where, grave thy victory?
  I triumph still, if Thou abide with me.

5 Hold Thou Thy Cross before my closing eyes,
  Shine through the gloom, and point me to the skies;
  Heaven's morning breaks, and earth's vain shadows flee:
  In life, in death, O Lord, abide with me!

Henry Francis Lyte, 1793-1847.

3 All hail King Jesus

Composer unknown
Arr. R. Fudge

All hail King Je-sus, all hail Em-man-u-el____ King of Kings, Lord of Lords, bright morn-ing star, ev-'ry-day you give me breath I'll sing your prai-ses____ and I'll reign with you through-out e-ter-ni-ty.____

4 All to Jesus I surrender

J.W. Van Deventer

W.S. Weeden
arr. R. Fudge

All to Je-sus I sur-ren-der, All to Him I free-ly give;
All to Je-sus I sur-ren-der, Hum-bly at His feet I bow,
All to Je-sus I sur-ren-der, Make me, Sav-iour, whol-ly Thine;
All to Je-sus I sur-ren-der, Lord, I give my-self to Thee;
All to Je-sus I sur-ren-der, Now I feel the sac-red flame;

I will ev-er love and trust Him, In His pres-ence dai-ly live.
World-ly plea-sures all for-sa-ken, Take me, Je-sus, take me now.
Let me feel the Ho-ly Spi-rit, Tru-ly know that Thou art mine.
Fill me with Thy love and pow-er, Let Thy bless-ing fall on me.
Oh, the joy of full sal-va-tion! Glo-ry, glo-ry to His name!

I sur-ren-der all, I sur-ren-der all,

All to Thee, my bless-ed Sav-iour, I sur-ren-der all.

5(i) All hail the power of Jesus' name

MILES LANE

W. Shrubsole

And crown Him, crown Him, crown Him, crown Him Lord of all.

1 All hail the power of Jesus' name!
　　Let angels prostrate fall;
　Bring forth the royal diadem,
　　And crown Him Lord of all.

2 Crown Him, ye martyrs of our God,
　　Who from His altar call;
　Extol the stem of Jesse's rod,
　　And crown Him Lord of all.

3 Ye seed of Israel's chosen race,
　　And ransomed from the fall,
　Hail Him who saves you by His grace,
　　And crown Him Lord of all.

4 Let every kindred, every tribe,
　　On this terrestrial ball,
　To Him all majesty ascribe,
　　And crown Him Lord of all.

5 O that with younder sacred throng
　　We at His feet may fall,
　Join in the everlasting song,
　　And crown Him Lord of all!

Edward Perronet, 1726-92.
John Rippon, 1751-1836.

5(ii)

DIADEM 8 6 8 6 extended

J. Ellor

crown him, him,

crown him, crown him,

crown him, crown him, crown him, crown

crown him, crown him, and crown him Lord of all.

6 All people that on earth do dwell

OLD HUNDREDTH 8 8 8 8 (L.M.)

Melody from Genevan Psalter 1551

1 All people that on earth do dwell,
   Sing to the Lord with cheerful voice:
   Him serve with mirth, His praise forth tell;
   Come ye before Him and rejoice.

2 The Lord, ye know, is God indeed;
   Without our aid He did us make:
   We are His folk, He doth us feed;
   And for His sheep He doth us take.

3 O enter then His gates with praise;
   Approach with joy His courts unto;
   Praise, laud, and bless His name always,
   For it is seemly so to do.

4 For why? The Lord our God is good;
   His mercy is for ever sure;
   His truth at all times firmly stood,
   And shall from age to age endure.

William Kethe, d. 1593 (?)

8

7 Alleluia

Anon.
arr. Betty Pulkingham

With quiet adoration

1. Al - le - lu - ia,___ Al - le - lu - ia,___ Al - le -

- lu - ia,___ Al - le - lu - ia.___ Al - le - lu - ia.___

2 How I love him

3 Blessed Jesus

4 My Redeemer

5 Jesus is Lord

6 Alleluia

8   All the riches of his grace

With simplicity, flowing

Jan Harrington

All the rich - es of his grace, all the ful - ness of his
bless-ings, all the sweet - ness of his love _ he gives to
you, _ he gives to me. All the me.

1. Oh, the blood of _ Je - sus, oh, the blood of _ Je - sus,
2. Oh, the word of _ Je - sus, oh, the word of _ Je - sus,
3. Oh, the love of _ Je - sus, oh, the love of _ Je - sus,

oh, the blood of _ Je - sus, it wash - es white as snow.
oh, the word of _ Je - sus, it clean-ses white as snow.
oh, the love of _ Je - sus, it makes his bo - dy

whole.

Oh, the blood of Je - sus,

whole. All the rich - es of his grace, all the

oh, the blood of Je - sus, oh, the blood of

ful - ness of his bless-ings, all the sweet - ness of his

Je - sus, it wash - es white as snow.

love he gives to you, _____ he gives to me.

9 Alleluia, alleluia, give thanks

ALLELUIA No. 1

Capo 3 (D)

Donald Fishel
Arr. Betty Pulkingham

REFRAIN
F(D)   Dm(Bm)   Gm(Em)   C(A)

Al - le - lu - ia, al-le-lu - ia, give_ thanks to the ris-en Lord. Al -le -

F(D)   Dm(Bm)   Gm(Em)   C(A)   *last time* F(D)

lu - ia, al-le-lu - ia, give_ praise to his _ name.

VERSES
F(D)   Dm(Bm)   Bb(G)   C(A)

1. Je - sus is Lord of all the _ earth.
2. Spread the good news o'er all the _ earth.
3. We have been cru - ci - fied with _ Christ.

F(D)   Dm(Bm)   Bb(G)   C(A)   *last time* F(D)

He is the King of cre - a - tion.   name.
Je - sus has died and has ris - en.   Al-le -
Now we shall live for ev - er.

4 God has proclaimed the just reward,
   Life for all men, alleluia.

5 Come let us praise the living God,
   Joyfully sing to our Saviour.

10   Amazing grace

Traditional
arr. Roland Fudge

AMAZING GRACE C.M.

1 Amazing grace! How sweet the sound
   That saved a wretch like me.
   I once was lost, but now am found,
   Was blind, but now I see.

2 'Twas grace that taught my heart to fear,
   And grace my fears relieved.
   How precious did that grace appear
   The hour I first believed.

3 Through many dangers, toils and snares,
   I have already come;
   'Tis grace hath brought me safe thus far,
   And grace will lead me home.

4 When we've been there ten thousand years,
   Bright shining as the sun,
   We've no less days to sing God's praise
   Than when we've first begun.

John Newton, 1725-1807

11 And can it be

SAGINA 88 88 88

Thomas Campbell (1825-76)

14

1 And can it be that I should gain
    An interest in the Saviour's blood?
Died He for me, who caused His pain?
    For me, who Him to death pursued?
Amazing love! how can it be
That Thou, my God, shouldst die for me!

2 'Tis mystery all! The Immortal dies:
    Who can explore His strange design?
In vain the first-born seraph tries
    To sound the depths of love divine.
'Tis mercy all! let earth adore,
Let angel minds inquire no more.

3 He left His Father's throne above —
    So free, so infinite His grace —
Emptied Himself of all but love,
    And bled for Adam's helpless race.
'Tis mercy all, immense and free;
For, O my God, it found out me!

4 Long my imprisoned spirit lay
    Fast bound in sin and nature's night;
Thine eye diffused a quickening ray —
    I woke, the dungeon flamed with light;
My chains fell off, my heart was free.
I rose, went forth, and followed Thee.

5 No condemnation now I dread;
    Jesus, and all in Him, is mine!
Alive in Him, my living Head,
    And clothed in righteousness divine,
Bold I approach the eternal throne,
And claim the crown, through Christ, my own.

Charles Wesley, 1707-88

12 Arise, shine

Adapted from Isaiah 60

Eric Glass
arr. Mimi Farra

With strength

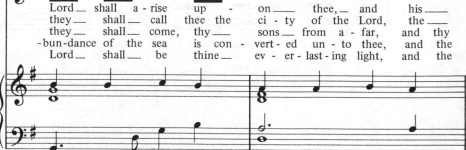

glo - ry shall be seen____ up - on thee.____
Zi - on of the Ho - ly One of Is - ra - el.____
daugh - ters shall be nursed__ at thy side.____
na - tions shall come__ un - to thee.____
days of thy mourn-ing shall be end - ed.____

REFRAIN

A - rise, shine; for thy light is come, and the

glo - ry of the Lord is ris - en.____ Oh, a - rise, shine; for thy

light is come, and the glo - ry of the Lord is up - on thee.____

13 As we are gathered

John Daniels
arr. Roland Fudge

As we are gathered, Jesus is here,
One with each other, Jesus is here,
Joined by the Spirit, washed in the blood,
Part of the body, the church of God,
As we are gathered, Jesus is here.
One with each other, Jesus is here.

14 Ascribe greatness

Composer unknown
arr. R. Fudge

As - cribe great-ness to our God the rock,___
As - cribe great-ness to our God the rock,___

___ his work is per - fect and all his ways are just ___
___ his work is per - fect and all his ways are just ___

___ A God of faith-ful - ness ___ and
___ A God of faith-ful - ness ___ and

with-out ___ in - just - ice, ___ good and up - right ___ is
with-out ___ in - just - ice, ___ good and

he. ___
up - right is he. ___

20

15(i) At the name of Jesus

EVELYNS 6 5 6 5 D

W.H. Monk

15(ii)

CAMBERWELL 6 5 6 5 D

Michael Brierley (1932-)

1 At the name of Jesus
  Every knee shall bow,
Every tongue confess Him
  King of glory now.
'Tis the Father's pleasure
  We should call Him Lord,
Who from the beginning
  Was the mighty Word:

2 Mighty and mysterious
  In the highest height,
God from everlasting,
  Very light of light.
In the Father's bosom,
  With the Spirit blest,
Love, in love eternal,
  Rest, in perfect rest.

3 Humbled for a season,
  To receive a name
From the lips of sinners
  Unto whom He came,
Faithfully He bore it
  Spotless to the last,
Brought it back victorious,
  When from death He passed;

4 Bore it up triumphant
  With its human light,
Through all ranks of creatures,
  To the central height;
To the throne of Godhead,
  To the Father's breast,
Filled it with the glory
  Of that perfect rest.

5 In your hearts enthrone Him;
  There let Him subdue
All that is not holy,
  All that is not true:
Crown Him as your captain
  In temptation's hour,
Let His will enfold you
  In its light and power.

6 Brothers, this Lord Jesus
  Shall return again,
With His Father's glory,
  With His angel-train;
For all wreaths of empire
  Meet upon His brow,
And our hearts confess Him
  King of glory now.

Caroline Noel, 1817-77

16 Be still and know

arr. Roland Fudge

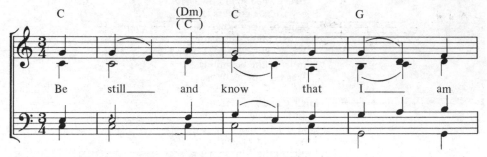

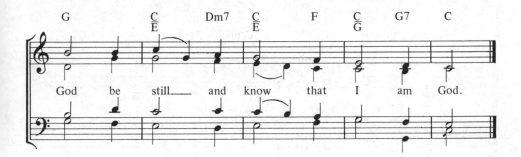

17 Be thou my vision

SLANE 10 10 10 10

Harmonized by Martin Shaw (1875–1958)

1 Be Thou my vision, O Lord of my heart;
Naught be all else to me, save that Thou art —
Thou my best thought, by day or by night,
Waking or sleeping, Thy presence my light.

2 Be Thou my Wisdom, Thou my true Word;
I ever with Thee, Thou with me, Lord;
Thou my great Father, I Thy true son;
Thou in me dwelling, and I with Thee one.

3 Be Thou my battle-shield, sword for the fight,
Be Thou my dignity, Thou my delight.
Thou my soul's shelter, Thou my high tower:
Raise Thou me heavenward,
    O Power of my power.

4 Riches I heed not, nor man's empty praise,
Thou mine inheritance, now and always:
Thou and Thou only, first in my heart,
High King of heaven, my treasure Thou art.

5 High King of heaven, after victory won,
May I reach heaven's joys,
    O bright heaven's Sun!
Heart of my own heart, whatever befall,
Still be my Vision, O Ruler of all.

Ancient Irish
tr. by Mary Elizabeth Byrne, 1880-1931
Versified by Eleanor Henrietta Hull

From *Enlarged Songs of Praise* by permission of Oxford University Press.

19 Because your love is better than life

Phil Potter
Arr. A. Maries

VERSES 2 - 4

F(E)
(v.3 ♩ ♩‿)

Gm(F♯m)

S.
A.

T.B.

2. Be-cause your   Son_____   has giv-en me   life
3. Be-cause your   Spi-rit_____   is fill-ing my   life   with my
4. Be-cause your   love_____   is bet-ter than   life

C(B7)

B♭(A)
F (E)   F(E)

F♯dim(Fdim)

lips   I will glo-ri-fy___ you, I will praise you__ as long as I

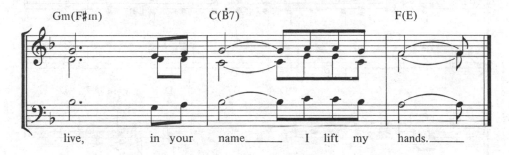

Gm(F♯m)   C(B7)   F(E)

live,   in your   name_____   I lift my   hands._____

Optional instrumental part:

(Voices)

20 Beneath the cross of Jesus

ST. CHRISTOPHER 7 6 8 6 8 6 8 6

Frederick Charles Maker

1 Beneath the Cross of Jesus
   I fain would take my stand —
The shadow of a mighty rock
   Within a weary land;
A home within a wilderness,
   A rest upon the way,
From the burning of the noontide heat
   And the burden of the day.

2 Upon that Cross of Jesus
   Mine eye at times can see
The very dying form of One
   Who suffered there for me.
And from my stricken heart, with tears,
   Two wonders I confess —
The wonders of redeeming love,
   And my own worthlessness.

3 I take, O Cross, thy shadow,
   For my abiding-place!
I ask no other sunshine than
   The sunshine of His face;
Content to let the world go by,
   To know no gain nor loss —
My sinful self my only shame,
   My glory all — the Cross.

Elizabeth Cecilia Clephane, 1836-69.

21 Bind us together Lord

B. Gillman
Arr. Norman Warren

Bind us to-geth-er Lord, bind us to-geth-er with (O)
cords that can-not be bro-ken; bind us to-geth-er with love!

1. There is on-ly one God, there is on-ly one King,
there is on-ly one Bo-dy that is why we sing:

2 Made for the glory of God,
   Purchased by His precious Son.
   Born with the right to be clean,
   For Jesus the victory has won.
   Bind us together....

3 You are the family of God.
   You are the promise divine.
   You are God's chosen desire.
   You are the glorious new wine.
   Bind us together....

Alternative words are at the end of this book

22 Blessed assurance

Irregular

Mrs. J.F. Knapp, 1839-1908

This is my sto - ry, this is my song,___ Prais-ing my

Sa - viour all the day long;___ This is my sto - ry, this is my

song, Prais-ing my Sa - viour all the day long.___

1 Blessed assurance, Jesus is mine:
   O what a foretaste of glory divine!
   Heir of salvation, purchase of God;
   Born of His Spirit, washed in His blood.
   This is my story, this is my song,
   Praising my Saviour all the day long.

2 Perfect submission, perfect delight,
   Visions of rapture burst on my sight;
   Angels descending, bring from above
   Echoes of mercy, whispers of love.

3 Perfect submission, all is at rest,
   I in my Saviour am happy and blest;
   Watching and waiting, looking above,
   Filled with His goodness, lost in His love.

Frances van Alstyne, 1820-1915

23 Break forth into joy

Anonymous
Arr. Roland Fudge

Break forth in-to joy O my soul, ___ Break forth in-to joy O my soul; In the pre-sence of the Lord there is joy for ev-er-more; Break forth, ___ break forth_in-to joy.

Arr. © 1983 Roland Fudge.

24 Bless the Lord, O my soul

BLESS THE LORD
Psalm 103
Capo 1

Andraé Crouch

34

25 Breathe on me breath of God

TRENTHAM S.M.

Capo 3 (D)

Robert Jackson

1 Breathe on me, Breath of God;
   Fill me with life anew.
That I may love what Thou dost love,
   And do what Thou wouldst do.

2 Breathe on me, Breath of God;
   Until my heart is pure,
Until with Thee I will one will,
   To do and to endure.

3 Breathe on me, Breath of God,
   Till I am wholly Thine,
Until this earthly part of me
   Glows with Thy fire divine.

4 Breathe on me, Breath of God;
   So shall I never die,
But live with Thee the perfect life
   Of Thine eternity.

Edwin Hatch (1835-89)

26 Bless the Lord, O my soul

Psalm 103

Composer unknown

Arr. R. Fudge

With breadth

Bless the Lord, O my soul, bless the Lord, O my

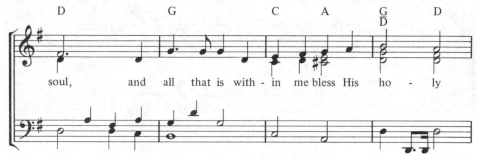

soul, and all that is with-in me bless His ho-ly

name, bless the Lord, O my soul, Bless the

Lord, O my soul and all that is with-

27 Christ is made the sure foundation

WESTMINSTER ABBEY 8 7 8 7 8 7   H. Purcell (1659-1695)

1 Christ is made the sure foundation,
  Christ the head and corner-stone
  Chosen of the Lord and precious,
  Binding all the Church in one;
  Holy Zion's help for ever,
  And her confidence alone.

2 All within that holy city
  Dearly loved of God on high,
  In exultant jubilation
  Sing, in perfect harmony;
  God the One-in-Three adoring
  In glad hymns eternally.

3 We as living stones invoke you:
  Come among us, Lord, today!
  With your gracious loving-kindness
  Hear your children as we pray;
  And the fulness of your blessing
  In our fellowship display.

4 Here entrust to all your servants
  What we long from you to gain —
  That on earth and in the heavens
  We one people shall remain,
  Till united in your glory
  Evermore with you we reign.

5 Praise and honour to the Father,
  Praise and honour to the Son,
  Praise and honour to the Spirit,
  Ever Three and ever One;
  One in power and one in glory
  While eternal ages run.

from the Latin (c. seventh century)
J.M. Neale (1818-1866)

© in this version *Jubilate Hymns*

28 Christ triumphant

M. Saward

M.A. Baughen

With triumphant vigour

Capo 3

Christ tri-um-phant ev-er reign-ing, Sav-iour, Mast-er, King,_____ Lord of heav'n, our lives sus-tain-ing, Hear us as we sing._____ Yours the glo-ry and the crown_____ The high re-nown_____ The e-ter-nal name._____

2 Word incarnate, truth revealing,
Son of Man on earth!
Power and majesty concealing
By your humble birth:
Yours the glory and the crown,
The high renown,
The eternal name.

3 Suffering servant, scorned, ill-treated,
Victim crucified!
Death is through the cross defeated,
Sinners justified:
Yours the glory and the crown,
The high renown,
The eternal name.

4 Priestly king, enthroned for ever
High in heaven above!
Sin and death and hell shall never
Stifle hymns of love:
Yours the glory and the crown,
The high renown,
The eternal name.

5 So, our hearts and voices raising
Through the ages long,
Ceaselessly upon you gazing,
This shall be our song:
Yours the glory and the crown,
The high renown,
The eternal name.

© Michael Saward (1932-   )

29 Christ is the answer

T.W. Maltby

Christ __ is the ans - wer to my ev - 'ry need;

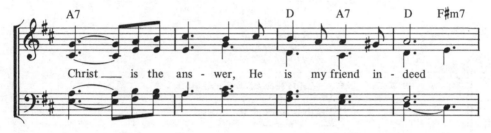

Christ __ is the ans - wer, He is my friend in - deed

Prob - lems of life my spi - rit may as - sail,

With Christ my Sav - iour I need nev - er fail, For

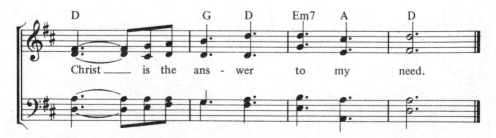

Christ __ is the ans - wer to my need.

30 Cleanse me from my sin

R. Hudson Pope

Cleanse me from my sin, Lord,— Put Thy pow'r with - in, Lord,

Take me as I— am, Lord, And make me all Thine own.—

Keep my day by day, Lord, Un - der-neath Thy sway, Lord,

Make my heart Thy pal - ace, and Thy roy - al throne.

31 Come and praise Him

With majesty

Capo 4 (C)

A. Carter

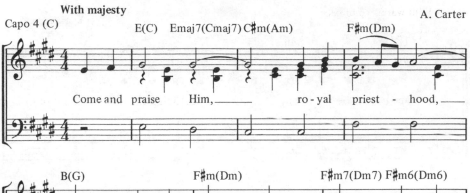

Come and praise Him,____ ro-yal priest-hood,____

Come and wor-ship,____ ho-ly

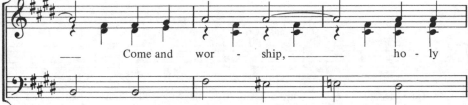

na - tion,____ Wor-ship Je - sus,____

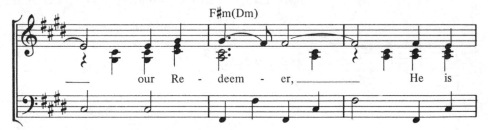

____ our Re-deem - er,____ He is

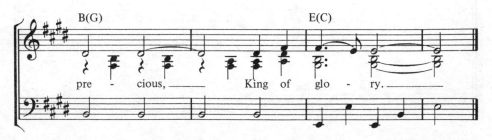

pre-cious,____ King of glo - ry.____

32 Come bless the Lord

With warmth and pace

Capo 1 (E)

arr. Margaret Evans

Come bless the Lord,_____ all ye ser-vants of the

Lord,_____ who stand by night_____

___ in the house of the Lord,_____ Lift up your

hands_____ in the ho - ly place,_____ Come bless the

Lord,_____ Come bless the Lord.

33 Come and see the shining hope

American traditional melody
arranged by David G. Wilson

MARCHING THROUGH GEORGIA 13 13 13 8 10 10 13 8

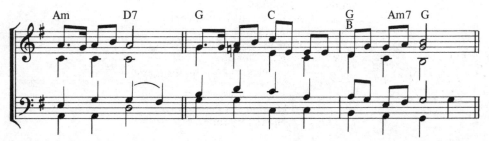

1 Come and see the shining hope
              that Christ's apostle saw;
On the earth, confusion,
              but in heaven an open door,
Where the living creatures
              praise the Lamb for evermore:
Love has the victory for ever!
       Amen, he comes! to bring his own reward!
       Amen, praise God! for justice now restored;
       Kingdoms of the world become
              the kingdoms of the Lord:
       Love has the victory for ever!

2 All the gifts you send us, Lord,
              are faithful, good, and true;
Holiness and righteousness
              are shown in all you do:
Who can see your greatest Gift
              and fail to worship you?
Love has the victory for ever!
       Amen, he comes! . . . .

3 Power and salvation
              all belong to God on high!
So the mighty multitudes of heaven
              make their cry,
Singing Alleluia!
              where the echoes never die:
Love has the victory for ever!
       Amen, he comes! . . . .

                          from Revelation 4-5 etc.

© Christopher Idle (1938-   )

34   Come down O Love Divine

DOWN AMPNEY 6 6 11 D

Ralph Vaughan Williams (1872-1958)

1   Come down, O Love Divine,
Seek Thou this soul of mine,
And visit it with Thine own ardour
glowing;
O Comforter, draw near,
Within my heart appear,
And kindle it Thy holy flame
bestowing.

2   O let it freely burn,
Till earthly passions turn
To dust and ashes, in its heat
consuming;
And let Thy glorious light
Shine ever on my sight,
And clothe me round, the while my
path illuming.

3   Let holy charity
Mine outward vesture be,
And lowliness become mine inner
clothing;
True lowliness of heart,
Which takes the humbler part,
And o'er its own shortcomings weeps
with loathing.

4   And so the yearning strong,
With which the soul will long,
Shall far outpass the power of human
telling;
For none can guess its grace,
Till he become the place
Wherein the Holy Spirit makes His
dwelling.

*Bianco da Siena, d. 1434;
tr. by Richard Frederick Littledale, 1833-90*

35 Come let us sing

WONDERFUL LOVE 10 4 10 7 4 10

F.L. Wiseman (1858-1944)

1 Come let us sing of a wonderful love,
    Tender and true;
  Out of the heart of the Father above,
    Streaming to me and to you:
      Wonderful love
  Dwells in the heart of the Father above.

2 Jesus, the Saviour, this gospel to tell,
    Joyfully came;
  Came with the helpless and hopeless to
      dwell,
    Sharing their sorrow and shame;
      Seeking the lost,
  Saving, redeeming at measureless cost.

3 Jesus is seeking the wanderers yet;
    Why do they roam?
  Love only waits to forgive and forget;
    Home! weary wanderers, home!
      Wonderful love
  Dwells in the heart of the Father above.

4 Come to my heart, O Thou wonderful
      love,
    Come and abide,
  Lifting my life till it rises above
    Envy and falsehood and pride;
      Seeking to be
  Lowly and humble, a learner of Thee.

Robert Walmsley, 1831-1905

49

36 Come, Holy Ghost

VENI CREATOR

arr. Roland Fudge

1 Come, Holy Ghost, our souls inspire,
  And lighten with celestial fire;
  Thou the anointing Spirit art,
  Who dost Thy sevenfold gifts impart:

2 Thy blessèd unction from above
  Is comfort, life, and fire of love;
  Enable with perpetual light
  The dullness of our blinded sight:

3 Anoint and cheer our soilèd face
  With the abundance of Thy grace:
  Keep far our foes, give peace at home;
  Where Thou art Guide no ill can come.

4 Teach us to know the Father, Son,
  And Thee, of both, to be but One;
  That through the ages all along
  This, this may be our endless song:

  Praise to Thy eternal merit,
  Father, Son, and Holy Spirit!

  Anonymous, 9th or 10th cent.;
  tr. by John Cosin (1594-1672)

37 Come let us join our cheerful songs

NATIVITY C.M.

H. Lahee, (1826-1912)

Capo 3

1 Come, let us join our cheerful songs
   With angels round the throne;
  Ten thousand thousand are their tongues,
   But all their joys are one.

2 "Worthy the Lamb that died!" they cry,
   "To be exalted thus";.
  "Worthy the Lamb!" our lips reply,
   "For He was slain for us."

3 Jesus is worthy to receive
   Honour and power divine;
  And blessings more than we can give
   Be, Lord, for ever Thine.

4 Let all that dwell above the sky,
   And air, and earth, and seas,
  Conspire to lift Thy glories high,
   And speak Thine endless praise.

5 The whole creation join in one,
   To bless the sacred name
  Of Him that sits upon the throne,
   And to adore the Lamb.

Isaac Watts, 1674-1748

38 Come to the waters

With a gentle swing

Jodi Page

Lyrics:

REFRAIN: Come to the wa-ters and you will be re-freshed. I will give you rest.

1. Je - sus said, 'Come un - to me that he gave, all ye who wea - ry, hea-vy la - den.'
2. Je - sus said, of the wa - ters that he gave, he who drinks shall nev - er thirst a - gain.
3. Je - sus said, 'He who be - lieves in me out of him shall flow liv - ing wa - ters.'
4. So with joy ye shall draw wa - ter out of wells of sal - va - tion.

39 Crown Him with many crowns

DIADEMATA D.S.M.   G.J. Elvey (1816-93)

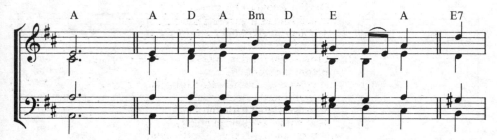

1   Crown Him with many crowns,
      The Lamb upon His throne;
Hark! how the heavenly anthem drowns
      All music but its own:
      Awake, my soul, and sing
      Of Him who died for thee,
And hail Him as thy chosen King
      Through all eternity.

2   Crown Him the Son of God
      Before the worlds began;
And ye who tread where He hath trod,
      Crown Him the Son of Man,
      Who every grief hath known
      That wrings the human breast,
And takes and bears them for His own,
      That all in Him may rest.

3   Crown Him the Lord of life,
      Who triumphed o'er the grave,
And rose victorious in the strife,
      For those He came to save:
      His glories now we sing,
      Who died and rose on high,
Who died eternal life to bring,
      And lives that death may die.

4   Crown Him the Lord of heaven,
      Enthroned in worlds above;
Crown Him the King to whom is given
      The wondrous name of love:
      All hail, Redeemer, hail!
      For Thou hast died for me;
Thy praise shall never, never fail
      Throughout eternity.

Matthew Bridges (1800-94)
Godfrey Thring (1823-1903)

40 Dear Lord and Father

REPTON 8 6 8 8 6 extended

C.H.H. Parry (1848-1918)

1 Dear Lord and Father of mankind,
    Forgive our foolish ways·
  Re-clothe us in our rightful mind;
  In purer lives Thy service find,
    In deeper reverence, praise.

2 In simple trust like theirs who heard,
    Beside the Syrian sea,
  The gracious calling of the Lord,
  Let us, like them, without a word
    Rise up and follow Thee.

3 O Sabbath rest by Galilee!
    O calm of hills above,
  Where Jesus knelt to share with Thee
  The silence of eternity,
    Interpreted by love!

4 With that deep hush subduing all
    Our words and works that drown
  The tender whisper of Thy call,
  As noiseless let Thy blessing fall
    As fell Thy manna down.

5 Drop Thy still dews of quietness,
    Till all our strivings cease;
  Take from our souls the strain and stress,
  And let our ordered lives confess
    The beauty of Thy peace.

6 Breathe through the heats of our desire
    Thy coolness and Thy balm;
  Let sense be dumb, let flesh retire;
  Speak through the earthquake, wind and fire,
    O still small voice of calm!

John Greenleaf Whittier (1807-82)

41 Do not be afraid

ISAIAH 43: i - 4.

Gerald Markland
arr. Roland Fudge

With warmth
INTRO. (optional)

CHORUS

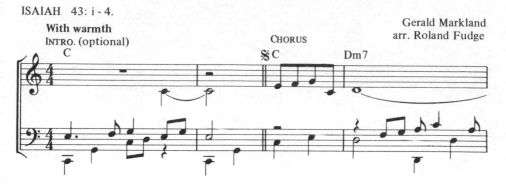

Do not be afraid, for I have redeemed you.
I have called you by your name; you are mine.

1 When you walk through the waters I'll be
   with you.
  You will never sink beneath the waves.

2 When the fire is burning all around you,
  You will never be consumed by the flames.

3 When the fear of loneliness is looming,
  Then remember I am at your side.

4 When you dwell in the exile of the
   stranger,
  Remember you are precious in my eyes.

5 You are mine, O my child; I am your
   Father,
  And I love you with a perfect love.

58

42 Do not be worried and upset

John 14:1–6   G. Taylor

VERSES

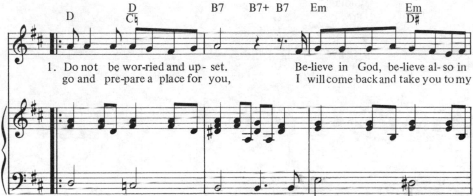

1. Do not be wor-ried and up-set. Be-lieve in God, be-lieve al-so in
go and pre-pare a place for you, I will come back and take you to my

me, There are ma-ny rooms in my Fa-ther's house, And I'm
self, So that you may come and be where I am. And I'm

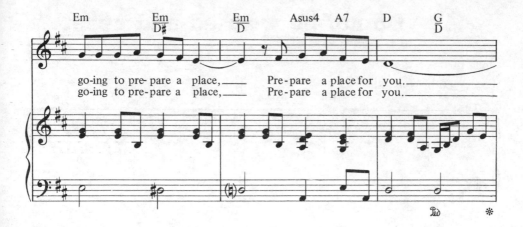

going to pre-pare a place,___ Pre-pare a place for you.___
going to pre-pare a place,___ Pre-pare a place for you.___

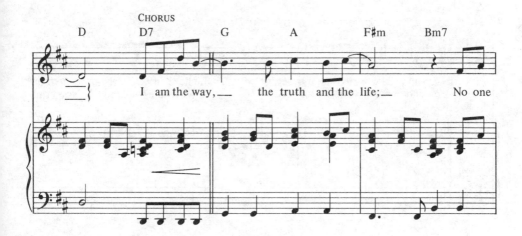

CHORUS

I am the way,___ the truth and the life;___ No one

goes to the Fa-ther ex-cept by me.__ I am the way, the truth and the

life, And I'm go-ing to pre-pare a place,___ Pre-pare a place for

you.___ 2. Af-ter I you. And I'm

go-ing to pre-pare a place,___ Pre-pare a place for you.

molto rall.

43 Father hear the prayer we offer

SUSSEX 8 7 8 7   coll. & adpt. Ralph Vaughan Williams (1872–1958)

1 Father, hear the prayer we offer:
  Not for ease that prayer shall be,
But for strength, that we may ever
  Live our lives courageously.

2 Not for ever in green pastures
  Do we ask our way to be:
But by steep and rugged pathways
  Would we strive to climb to Thee.

3 Not for ever by still waters
  Would we idly quiet stay;
But would smite the living fountains
  From the rocks along our way.

4 Be our strength in hours of weakness,
  In our wanderings be our guide;
Through endeavour, failure, danger,
  Father, be Thou at our side.

5 Let our path be bright or dreary,
  Storm or sunshine be our share;
May our souls, in hope unweary,
  Make Thy work our ceaseless prayer.

Love Maria Willis, 1824-1908

44 Father, we adore You

Terrye Coelho

Can be sung as a 3-part round

1 Father, we adore you,
   Lay our lives before you:
   How we love you!

2 Jesus, we adore you,
   Lay our lives before you:
   How we love you!

3 Spirit, we adore you,
   Lay our lives before you:
   How we love you!

45 Father, I place into your hands

Prayerfully

J. Hewer

1 Father, I place into your hands
   The things that I can't do.
   Father, I place into your hands
   The times that I've been through.
   Father, I place into your hands
   The way that I should go,
   For I know I always can trust you.

2 Father, I place into your hands
   My friends and family.
   Father, I place into your hands
   The things that trouble me.
   Father, I place into your hands
   The person I would be,
   For I know I always can trust you.

3 Father, we love to seek your face,
   We love to hear your voice.
   Father, we love to sing your praise,
   And in your name rejoice.
   Father, we love to walk with you
   And in your presence rest,
   For we know we always can trust you.

4 Father, I want to be with you
   And do the things you do.
   Father, I want to speak the words
   That you are speaking too.
   Father, I want to love the ones
   That you will draw to you,
   For I know that I am one with you.

46 Father, we love You

Quite slow

Donna Adkins

1. Fa - ther, we love You, we wor - ship and a - dore You,
2. Je - sus, we love You, we wor - ship and a - dore You,
3. Spi - rit, we love You, we wor - ship and a - dore You,

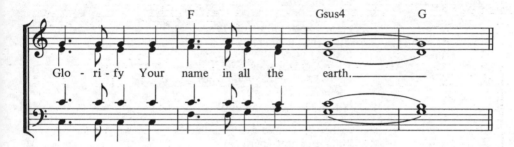

Glo - ri - fy Your name in all the earth.

Glo - ri - fy Your name, Glo - ri - fy Your name,

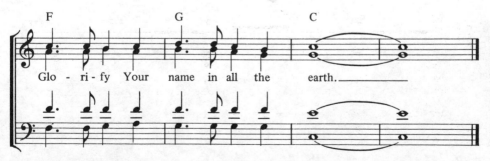

Glo - ri - fy Your name in all the earth.

47 Fear not! Rejoice and be glad

Adapted from Joel 2,3,4

Priscilla Wright

Fear not, re-joice and be glad, the Lord hath done a great thing; hath poured out his Spi-rit on all man-kind, on those who con-fess his name.

1. The fig tree is bud-ding, the vine bear-eth fruit, the wheat fields are gold-en with grain. Thrust in the sic-kle, the har-vest is ripe, the Lord has giv-en us rain.
2. Ye shall eat in plen-ty and be sat-is-fied, the moun-tains will drip with sweet wine. My chil-dren shall drink of the foun-tain of life, my chil-dren will know they are mine.
3. My peo-ple shall know that I am the Lord, their shame I have tak-en a-way. My Spi-rit will lead them to-geth-er a-gain, my Spi-rit will show them the way.
4. My chil-dren shall dwell in a bo-dy of love, a light to the world they will be. Life shall come forth from the Fa-ther a-bove, my bo-dy will set man-kind free.

48(i) Fill thou my life

ST. FULBERT C.M.

H.J. Gauntlett (1805-76)

1 Fill Thou my life, O Lord my God,
   In every part with praise,
  That my whole being may proclaim
   Thy being and Thy ways.

2 Not for the lip of praise alone,
   Nor e'en the praising heart,
  I ask, but for a life made up
   Of praise in every part:

3 Praise in the common things of life,
   Its goings out and in;
  Praise in each duty and each deed,
   However small and mean.

4 Fill every part of me with praise;
   Let all my being speak
  Of Thee and of Thy love, O Lord,
   Poor though I be and weak.

5 So shalt Thou, Lord, from me, e'en me,
   Receive the glory due;
  And so shall I begin on earth
   The song for ever new.

6 So shall no part of day or night
   From sacredness be free;
  But all my life, in every step,
   Be fellowship with Thee.

Horatius Bonar, 1808-82

48(ii)

Adapted from T. Hawels (1734-1820)
by S. Webbe (the younger)

RICHMOND C.M.

49 Fight the good fight

DUKE STREET (L.M.)

J. Hatton (*d.* 1793)

1 Fight the good fight with all thy might;
  Christ is thy strength, and Christ thy right;
  Lay hold on life, and it shall be
  Thy joy and crown eternally.

2 Run the straight race through God's good grace;
  Lift up thine eyes, and seek His face,
  Life with its path before thee lies;
  Christ is the way, and Christ the prize.

3 Cast care aside, lean on thy Guide,
  His boundless mercy will provide;
  Lean, and thy trusting soul shall prove,
  Christ is thy life, and Christ thy love.

4 Faint not, nor fear, His arm is near,
  He changeth not, and thou art dear,
  Only believe, and thou shalt see
  That Christ is all in all to thee.

John Samuel Bewley Monsell, 1811-75

50 For I'm building a people of power

D. Richards

Brightly

For I'm build-ing a peo-ple of pow-er__ And I'm mak-ing a peo-ple of

praise, That will move thro' this land by My Spi-rit, __ And will

glo-ri-fy my pre-cious Name. Build Your Church, Lord, Make us

strong, Lord, Join our hearts, Lord, through Your Son Make us

one, Lord, in Your Bo-dy, In the King-dom of Your Son. __

51 For all the saints

SINE NOMINE 10 10 10 4

Ralph Vaughan Williams (1872-1958)

1 For all the saints who from their labours rest,
Who Thee by faith before the world confessed,
Thy name, O Jesu, be for ever blest.
Alleluia!

2 Thou wast their Rock, their Fortress, and their Might;
Thou, Lord, their Captain in the well fought fight;
Thou in the darkness drear their one true Light.
Alleluia!

3 O may Thy soldiers, faithful, true, and bold,
Fight as the saints who nobly fought of old,
And win, with them, the victor's crown of gold!
Alleluia!

4 O blest communion, fellowship divine!
We feebly struggle; they in glory shine,
Yet all are one in Thee, for all are Thine.
Alleluia!

5 And when the strife is fierce, the warfare long,
Steals on the ear the distant triumph song,
And hearts are brave again, and arms are strong.
Alleluia!

6 The golden evening brightens in the west;
Soon, soon to faithful warriors cometh rest;
Sweet is the calm of paradise the blest.
Alleluia!

7 But lo! there breaks a yet more glorious day:
The saints triumphant rise in bright array;
The King of Glory passes on His way.
Alleluia!

8 From earth's wide bounds, from ocean's farthest coast,
Through gates of pearl streams in the countless host,
Singing to Father, Son, and Holy Ghost:
Alleluia!

William Walsham How, 1823-97

52 For the fruits of His creation

EAST ACKLAM 8 4 8 4 8 8 8 4

Francis Jackson (1917-   )

Capo 3

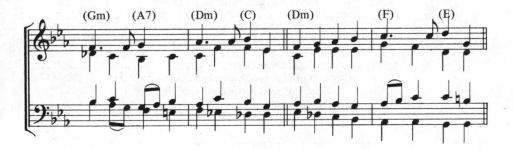

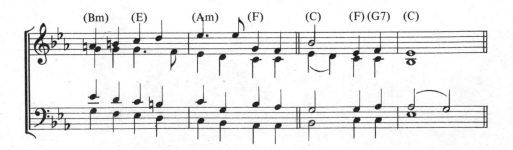

1 For the fruits of his creation,
    Thanks be to God!
For his gifts to every nation,
    Thanks be to God!
For the ploughing, sowing, reaping,
Silent growth while we are sleeping;
Future needs in earth's safe seeking,
    Thanks be to God!

2 In the just reward of labour,
    God's will is done;
In the help we give our neighbour,
    God's will is done;
In our worldwide task of caring
For the hungry and despairing;
In the harvests we are sharing,
    God's will is done.

3 For the harvests of the Spirit,
    Thanks be to God!
For the good we all inherit,
    Thanks be to God!
For the wonders that astound us,
For the truths that still confound us;
Most of all, that love has found us,
    Thanks be to God!

F. Pratt Green 1903-
© *Stainer & Bell*

53 For Thou, O Lord

Pete Sanchez Jr.

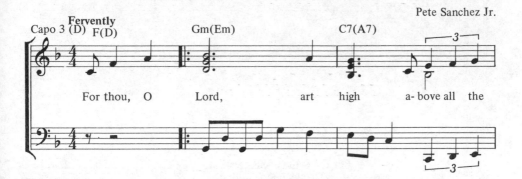

For thou, O   Lord,   art high   a- bove all the

earth,_____   Thou art ex - al - ted   far a-

bove   all__ gods_____   for thou, O

bove   all   gods._____   I ex -

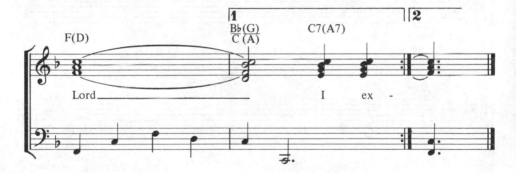

54 From the rising of the sun

Psalm 113:3.1.2.

Paul Deming

From the ris-ing of the sun to the go-ing down of the same the Lord's name is to be praised. From the ris-ing of the Praise ye the Lord,

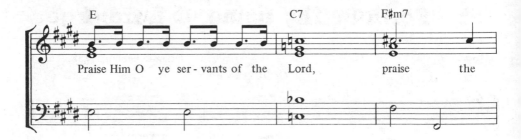

Praise Him O ye ser - vants of the Lord, praise the

name of the Lord, bles - sed be the

name of the Lord from this time forth,

and for ev - er - more.

55 Forth in Thy name, O Lord, I go

ANGELS' SONG 8 8 8 8 (L.M.)   Orlando Gibbons (1583-1625)

1 Forth in Thy name, O Lord, I go,
   My daily labour to pursue,
 Thee, only Thee, resolved to know
   In all I think, or speak, or do.

2 The task Thy wisdom hath assigned
   O let me cheerfully fulfil,.
 In all my works Thy presence find,
   And prove Thy acceptable will.

3 Thee may I set at my right hand,
   Whose eyes my inmost substance see,
 And labour on at Thy command,
   And offer all my works to Thee.

4 Give me to bear Thy easy yoke,
   And every moment watch and pray,
 And still to things eternal look,
   And hasten to Thy glorious day:

5 For Thee delightfully employ
   Whate'er Thy bounteous grace hath given,
 And run my course with even joy,
   And closely walk with Thee to heaven.

Charles Wesley, 1707-88

56 Father God, I love you

FATHER GOD

Joan Robinson

Gently

1 Father God, I love you
  Father God, I love you
  Father God, I love you
  Come into my life.

2 Jesus, I love you
  Jesus, I love you
  Jesus, I love you
  Come into my life.

3 Spirit, I love you
  Spirit, I love you
  Spirit, I love you
  Come into my life.

4 Alleluia
  Alleluia
  Alleluia
  Alleluia.

Repeat last verse

57   Give me a sight, O Saviour

Words and Music Katherine Agnes May Kelly (1869-1942)

1. Give me a sight, O Sav-iour, Of Thy
2. Was it the nails, O Sav-iour, That __
3. O won-der of all won-ders, That __
4. Then melt my heart, O Sav-iour, Bend me,

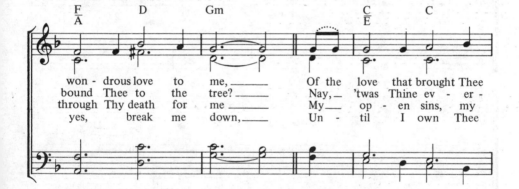

won-drous love to me, __ Of the love that brought Thee
bound Thee to the tree? __ Nay, __ 'twas Thine ev-er-
through Thy death for me __ My __ op-en sins, my
yes, break me down, __ Un-til I own Thee

down to earth, To die on Cal-va-ry. __
-last-ing love, Thy love for me, for me. __
se-cret sins, Can all for-giv-en be! __
Con-que-ror, And Lord and Sov-ereign crown. __

O make me un - der - stand it,

Help me to take it in,_____ What it meant to Thee, the

Ho - ly One, To bear___ a - way my sin._____

58 Give me oil in my lamp

Anon

Arr. Betty Pulkingham

1. Give me oil in my lamp, keep me burn-ing._____ Give me
2. Make me a fish - er of men, keep me seek - ing._____ Make me a
3. Give me joy in my heart, keep me sing - ing._____ Give me
4. Give me love in my heart, keep me serv - ing._____ Give me

oil in my lamp, I pray. Give me
fish - er of men, I pray. Make me a
joy in my heart, I pray. Give me
love in my heart, I pray. Give me

oil in my lamp, keep me burn - ing,_____ keep me
fish - er of men, keep me seek - ing,_____ keep me
joy in my heart, keep me sing - ing,_____ keep me
love in my heart, keep me serv - ing,_____ keep me

84

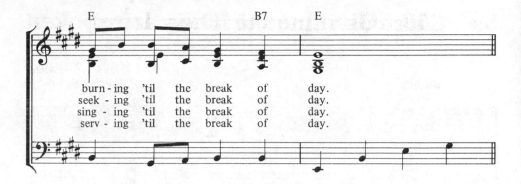

burn - ing 'til the break of day.
seek - ing 'til the break of day.
sing - ing 'til the break of day.
serv - ing 'til the break of day.

Chorus

Sing ho-san - na, sing ho-san - na,

sing ho-san - na to the King of Kings! King! 2. Make

59 Glorious things of Thee are spoken

AUSTRIA 8 7 8 7 D

Croatian Folk-tune, adapted by
F.J. Haydn (1732-1809)

1 Glorious things of thee are spoken,
    Zion, city of our God;
He, whose word cannot be broken,
    Formed thee for His own abode.
On the Rock of Ages founded,
    What can shake thy sure repose?
With salvation's walls surrounded,
    Thou may'st smile at all thy foes.

2 See, the streams of living waters,
    Springing from eternal love,
Well supply thy sons and daughters
    And all fear of want remove:
Who can faint, while such a river
    Ever flows their thirst to assuage?
Grace which, like the Lord, the Giver
    Never fails from age to age.

3 Saviour, if of Zion's city
    I, through grace, a member am,
Let the word deride or pity,
    I will glory in Thy name:
Fading is the worldling's pleasure,
    All his boasted pomp and show:
Solid joys and lasting treasure
    None but Zion's children know.

John Newton, 1725-1807

60 God forgave my sin

Carol Owens

Smoothly

1. God for - gave my sin in Je - sus'
   pow'r is giv'n in Je - sus'

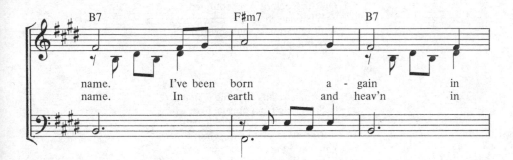

name. I've been born a - gain in
name. In earth and heav'n in

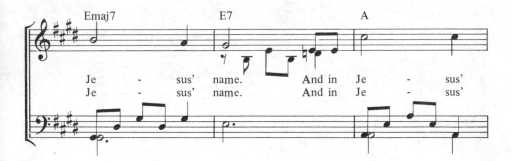

Je - sus' name. And in Je - sus'
Je - sus' name. And in Je - sus'

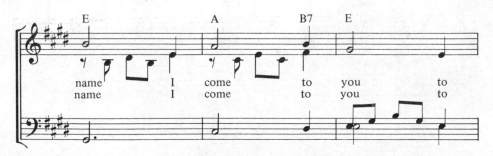

name I come to you to
name I come to you to

Freely, Freely, Words and Music Carol Owens
© 1972 Lexicon Music Inc., Word Music (U.K.),
Northbridge Road, Berkhamsted, Herts, HP4 1EH

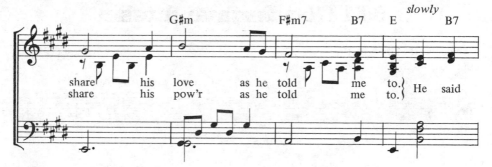

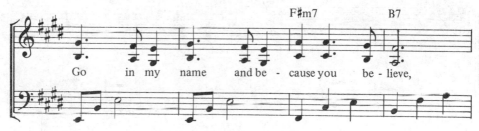

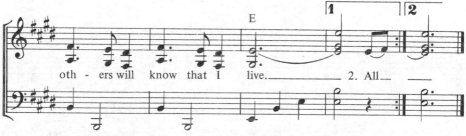

*For variation, some voices may sing in thirds above the refrain melody, like this:

etc.

61 Go forth and tell

YANWORTH 10 10 10 10

Capo 3

John Barnard (1948 -)

1 Go forth and tell! O Church of God,
    awake!
God's saving news to all the nations
    take:
Proclaim Christ Jesus, saviour, Lord,
    and king,
That all the world his worthy praise
    may sing.

2 Go forth and tell! God's love embraces
    all;
He will in grace respond to all who call:
How shall they call if they have never
    heard
The gracious invitation of his word?

3 Go forth and tell! Men still in darkness
    lie;
In wealth or want, in sin they live
    and die:
Give us, O Lord, concern of heart
    and mind,
A love like yours which cares for all
    mankind.

4 Go forth and tell! The doors are open
    wide:
Share God's good gifts — let no one be
    denied;
Live out your life as Christ your Lord
    shall choose,
Your ransomed powers for his sole
    glory use.

5 Go forth and tell! O church of God,
    arise!
Go in the strength which Christ your
    Lord supplies;
Go till all nations his great name adore
And serve him, Lord and king for
    evermore.

© *James E. Seddon 1915-*

62 Great is Thy faithfulness

11 10 11 10 and refrain

W.M. Runyan (1870-1957)

1 Great is Thy faithfulness, O God my
    Father,
  There is no shadow of turning with
    Thee;
  Thou changest not, Thy compassions
    they fail not,
  As Thou hast been Thou for ever wilt
    be.

  Great is Thy faithfulness!
  Great is Thy faithfulness!
  Morning by morning new mercies
    I see;
  All I have needed Thy hand hath
    provided, —
  Great is Thy faithfulness, Lord,
    unto me!

2 Summer and winter, and spring-time
    and harvest,
  Sun, moon and stars in their courses
    above,
  Join with all nature in manifold witness
  To Thy great faithfulness, mercy and
    love.

3 Pardon for sin and a peace that
    endureth,
  Thine own dear presence to cheer and
    to guide;
  Strength for today and bright hope for
    tomorrow,
  Blessings all mine, with ten thousand
    beside!

T.O. Chisholm, 1866-1960

63 Guide me, O Thou great Jehovah

CWM RHONDDA 8 7 8 7 4 7 extended

J. Hughes (1873-1932)

1 Guide me, O Thou great Jehovah,
    Pilgrim through this barren land;
I am weak, but Thou art mighty;
    Hold me with Thy powerful hand:
      Bread of heaven,
    Feed me now and evermore.

2 Open now the crystal fountain,
    Whence the healing stream doth flow;
Let the fiery, cloudy pillar
    Lead me all my journey through:
      Strong deliverer,
    Be Thou still my strength and shield.

3 When I tread the verge of Jordan,
    Bid my anxious fears subside:
Death of death, and hell's destruction,
    Land me safe on Canaan's side:
      Songs of praises
    I will ever give to Thee.

William Williams, 1717-91, altd.

64 Hail to the Lord's anointed

CRUGER 7 6 7 6 D

J. Crüger (1598-1662)

Capo 3

1 Hail to the Lord's Anointed;
    Great David's greater Son!
Hail, in the time appointed,
    His reign on earth begun!
He comes to break oppression,
    To set the captive free,
To take away transgression,
    And rule in equity.

2 He comes, with succour speedy,
    To those who suffer wrong;
To help the poor and needy,
    And bid the weak be strong:
To give them songs for sighing,
    Their darkness turn to light,
Whose souls, condemned and dying,
    Were precious in His sight.

3 He shall come down like showers
    Upon the fruitful earth:
Love, joy, and hope, like flowers,
    Spring in His path to birth:
Before Him, on the mountains,
    Shall peace the herald go;
And righteousness in fountains,
    From hill to valley flow.

4 Kings shall fall down before Him,
    And gold and incense bring;
All nations shall adore Him,
    His praise all people sing;
To Him shall prayer unceasing
    And daily vows ascend;
His kingdom still increasing,
    A kingdom without end.

5 O'er every foe victorious,
    He on His throne shall rest;
From age to age more glorious,
    All-blessing and all-blest.
The tide of time shall never
    His covenant remove;
His name shall stand for ever
    His changeless name of Love.

James Montgomery, 1771-1854

65 Hallelujah! For the Lord our God

Triumphantly

D. Garrett

Hal-le-lu-jah, _ for the Lord our God the Al-migh-ty_ reigns._ Hal-le-reigns. Let us re-joice_ and be glad_ and give the glo-ry un-to Him._ Hal-le-lu-jah, for_ the Lord our God the Al-migh-ty_ reigns._

98

66 Hallelujah, my Father

With quiet devotion

Tim Cullen

Hal-le-lu-jah, my Fa - ther, for giv-ing us your Son;

send-ing him in to the world to be giv-en up for men,

know-ing we would bruise him and smite him from the earth. Hal-le-

lu - jah, my Fa - ther, in his death is my birth. Hal-le-

lu - jah, my Fa - ther, in his life is my life.

67 Hallelujah sing to Jesus

HALLELUJAH 87 87 D

S.S. Wesley (1810-76)

1 Hallelujah! sing to Jesus,
    His the sceptre, His the throne;
  Hallelujah! His the triumph,
    His the victory alone;
  Hark! the songs of peaceful Sion
    Thunder like a mighty flood;
  Jesus out of every nation
    Hath redeemed us by His blood.

2 Hallelujah! not as orphans
    Are we left in sorrow now;
  Hallelujah! He is near us,
    Faith believes, nor questions how:
  Though the cloud from sight received Him
    When the forty days were o'er,
  Shall our hearts forget His promise,
    "I am with you evermore"?

3 Hallelujah! bread of angels,
    Thou on earth our food, our stay;
  Hallelujah! here the sinful
    Flee to Thee from day to day;
  Intercessor, friend of sinners,
    Earth's Redeemer, plead for me,
  Where the songs of all the sinless
    Sweep across the crystal sea.

4 Hallelujah! Hallelujah!
    Glory be to God on high;
  To the Father, and the Saviour,
    Who has gained the victory;
  Glory to the Holy Spirit,
    Fount of love and sanctity.
  Hallelujah! Hallelujah!
    To the triune Majesty.

W.C. Dix, 1837-98, altd.

68 He is here, He is here

Jimmy Owens
arr. Roland Fudge

1. He is here, he is here, he is mov-ing a-mong us; he is here, he is here, as we ga-ther in his name! He is here, he is here, and he wants to work a won-der; he is here as we ga-ther in his

2. He is Lord, he is Lord, let us wor-ship be-fore him; he is Lord, he is Lord, as we ga-ther in his name! He is Lord, he is Lord, let us

name.

praise and a -dore him—yes-ter-

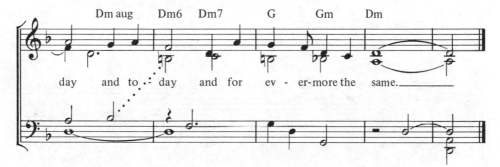

day and to day and for ev - er-more the same.

69 He is Lord

author unknown
arranged Roland Fudge

He is Lord. _____ he is Lord. _____ He is
ris - en from the dead, and he is Lord. _____ Ev - 'ry
knee shall bow, ev - 'ry tongue con - fess that
Je - sus Christ is Lord. _____

70 His hands were pierced

From "The Victorious Christ."

D. Wood

1. His Hands were pierced,— the Hands that made The moun - tain
2. His Feet were pierced,— the Feet that trod The fur - thest

range — and ev - er - glade; That washed — the stains of
shin - ing star — of God; And left — their im - print

sin — a - way And changed earth's dark - ness in - to day.
deep — and clear On ev - 'ry wind - ing path - way here.

3 His Heart was pierced, the Heart that burned
  To comfort every heart that yearned!
  And from it came a cleansing flood,
  The river of redeeming Blood.

4 His Hands and Feet and Heart, all three
  Were pierced for me on Calvary,
  And here and now, to Him I bring
  My hands, feet, heart, an offering.

71 His name is higher

author unknown
arranged Margaret Evans

With majesty

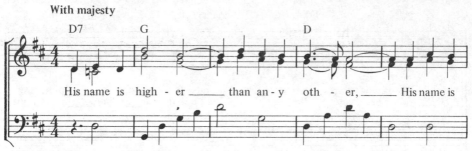

His name is high - er _____ than an - y oth - er, _____ His name is

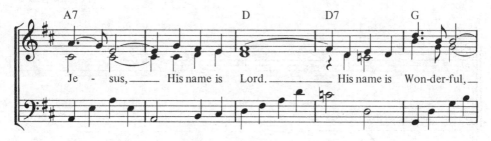

Je - sus, _____ His name is Lord. _____ His name is Won-der-ful, _____

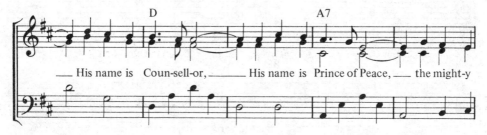

_____ His name is Coun-sell-or, _____ His name is Prince of Peace, _____ the might-y

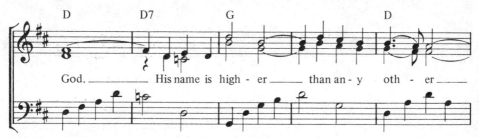

God. _____ His name is high - er _____ than an - y oth - er _____

_____ His name is Je - sus, _____ His name is Lord. _____

72   His name is wonderful

Words and Music by Audrey Mieir
Arr. Norman Warren

His name is won-der-ful, his name is won-der-ful,
He is the might-y king, mas-ter of ev-ery-thing,
His name is won-der-ful, Je-sus my Lord;
Je-sus my Lord. He's the great shep-herd, the rock of all a-ges,
al-might-y God is he; _____ bow down be-fore him,
love and a-dore him, His name is won-der-ful, Je-sus my Lord!

73 Holy, Holy, Holy

NICAEA 11 12 12 10

J.B. Dykes (1823-1876)

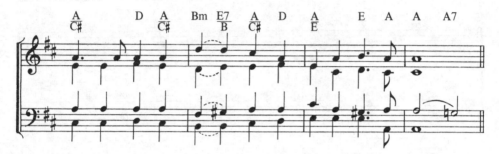

1 Holy, holy, holy, Lord God almighty!
   Early in the morning our song shall rise to Thee;
   Holy, holy, holy, merciful and mighty,
   God in three Persons, blessèd Trinity!

2 Holy, holy, holy! all the saints adore Thee,
   Casting down their golden crowns around the glassy sea;
   Cherubim and seraphim falling down before Thee,
   Who wast, and art, and evermore shalt be.

3 Holy, holy, holy! though the darkness hide Thee,
   Though the eye of sinful man Thy glory may not see,
   Only Thou art holy; there is none beside Thee,
   Perfect in power, in love, and purity.

4 Holy, holy, holy, Lord God almighty!
   All Thy works shall praise Thy name, in earth, and sky,
       and sea:
   Holy, holy, holy, merciful and mighty,
   God in three Persons, blessèd Trinity!

Reginald Heber, 1783-1826

74 Holy, Holy, Holy is the Lord

Unknown
Arr. Norman Warren

1. Ho - ly, ho - ly, ho - ly is the Lord; ho - ly is the
2. Je - sus, Je - sus, Je - sus is the Lord; Je - sus is the
3. Wor - thy, wor - thy, wor - thy is the Lord; wor - thy is the
4. Glo - ry, glo - ry, glo - ry to the Lord; glo - ry to the

Lord God al - migh - ty!
Lord God al - migh - ty, ty,
Lord God al - migh - ty!
Lord God al - migh - ty, who was, and is, and is to

come: ho - ly, ho - ly, ho - ly is the Lord! _

110

75 Holy, Holy

Words and Music Jimmy Owens

Ho-ly, ho - ly, ho-ly, ho-ly, ho-ly, ho - ly__ Lord God al-

migh-ty! And we lift our hearts be-fore__ you as a to-ken of our love: ho-ly,

ho - ly, ho-ly, ho - ly.

2 Gracious Father, gracious Father,
   We're so glad to be your children,
       gracious Father;
   And we lift our heads before you
   As a token of our love,
   Gracious Father, gracious Father.

3 Precious Jesus, precious Jesus,
   We're so glad that you've redeemed us,
       precious Jesus;
   And we lift our hands before you
   As a token of our love,
   Precious Jesus, precious Jesus.

4 Holy Spirit, Holy Spirit,
   Come and fill our hearts anew, Holy
       Spirit! —
   And we lift our voice before you
   As a token of our love,
   Holy Spirit, Holy Spirit.

5 Hallelujah, hallelujah,
   Hallelujah, hallelujah —
   And we lift our hearts before you
   As a token of our love
   Hallelujah, hallelujah.

111

76 How firm a foundation

MONTGOMERY 11 11 11 11

Probably by S. Jarvis (died *c.* 1785)

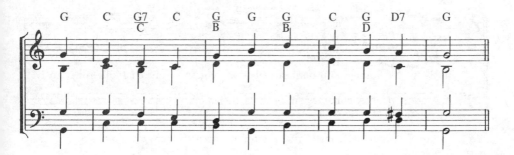

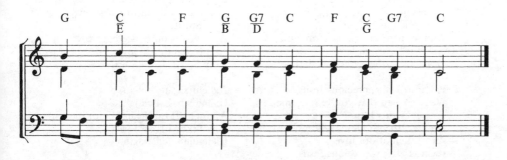

1 How firm a foundation, ye saints of the Lord,
   Is laid for your faith in His excellent word:
   What more can He say than to you He hath said,
   You who unto Jesus for refuge have fled?

2 Fear not, He is with thee, O be not dismayed;
   For He is thy God, and will still give thee aid:
   He'll strengthen thee, help thee, and cause thee to stand,
   Upheld by His righteous, omnipotent hand.

3 In every condition, in sickness, in health,
   In poverty's vale, or abounding in wealth;
   At home and abroad, on the land, on the sea,
   As thy days may demand shall thy strength ever be.

4 When through the deep waters He calls thee to go,
   The rivers of grief shall not thee overflow;
   For He will be with thee in trouble to bless,
   And sanctify to thee thy deepest distress.

5 When through fiery trials thy pathway shall lie,
   His grace all-sufficient shall be thy supply;
   The flame shall not hurt thee, His only design
   Thy dross to consume and thy gold to refine.

6 The soul that on Jesus has leaned for repose
   He will not, He will not, desert to its foes;
   That soul, though all hell should endeavour to shake,
   He'll never, no never, no never forsake.

"K" in Rippon's *Selection*, 1787, *altd.*

77 How good is the God we adore

CELESTE 8 8 8 8 (L.M.)   Lancashire Sunday School Songs 1857

1 How good is the God we adore!
  Our faithful, unchangeable friend:
  His love is as great as his power
  And knows neither measure nor end.

2 For Christ is the first and the last;
  His Spirit will guide us safe home:
  We'll praise him for all that is past
  And trust him for all that's to come.

J. Hart, 1712-1768

78 How sweet the name of Jesus

ST. PETER 8 6 8 6 (C.M.)

A.R. Reinagle (1799-1877)

1 How sweet the name of Jesus sounds
    In a believer's ear!
It soothes his sorrows, heals his wounds,
    And drives away his fear.

2 It makes the wounded spirit whole,
    And calms the troubled breast;
'Tis manna to the hungry soul,
    And to the weary rest.

3 Dear name! the rock on which I build,
    My shield and hiding-place,
My never-failing treasury, filled
    With boundless stores of grace.

4 Jesus! my shepherd, brother, friend,
    My prophet, priest, and king;
My lord, my life, my way, my end,
    Accept the praise I bring.

5 Weak is the effort of my heart,
    And cold my warmest thought;
But when I see Thee as Thou art,
    I'll praise Thee as I ought.

6 Till then I would Thy love proclaim
    With every fleeting breath;
And may the music of Thy name
    Refresh my soul in death!

John Newton, 1725-1807, altd.

79 How lovely on the mountains

OUR GOD REIGNS

Triumphantly with pace

L. E. Smith Jnr.

Capo 1 (A)

1. How love-ly on the moun-tains are the feet of Him Who brings good news,_____ good news, Pro-claim-ing peace, an-nounc-ing news of hap-pi-ness,_____ Our God reigns_____ Our God reigns._____ Our God reigns_____ Our God reigns_____

[orig. version] An-nounc-ing peace, pro-claim-ing news of hap-pi - ness,

[orig. version] Saying to Zi - on: Your God reigns.

[orig. version] Your God reigns Your God reigns

Our God reigns____ ____ Our God reigns.____

[orig. version] *Your God reigns* *Your God reigns.*

Popular Version

2 You watchmen lift your voices joyfully as one,
  Shout for your King, your King.
  See eye to eye the Lord restoring Zion:
  Your God reigns, your God reigns!

3 Waste places of Jerusalem break forth with joy,
  We are redeemed, redeemed.
  The Lord has saved and comforted His people:
  Your God reigns, your God reigns!

4 Ends of the earth, see the salvation of your God,
  Jesus is Lord, is Lord.
  Before the nations He has bared His holy arm:
  Your God reigns, your God reigns!

Original Version

2 He had no stately form, He had no majesty,
  That we should be — drawn to Him.
  He was despised and we took no account of Him,
  Yet now He reigns — with the Most High.
      Chorus: Now He reigns   *(three times)*
             With the Most High!

3 It was our sin and guilt that bruised and wounded Him,
  It was our sin — that brought Him down.
  When we like sheep had gone astray, our Shepherd came
  And on His shoulders — bore our shame.
      Chorus: On His shoulders   *(three times)*
             He bore our shame.

4 Meek as a lamb that's led out to the slaughterhouse,
  Dumb as a sheep — before its shearer,
  His life ran down upon the ground like pouring rain,
  That we might be — born again.
      Chorus: That we might be   *(three times)*
             Born again.

5 Out from the tomb He came with grace and majesty,
  He is alive — He is alive.
  God loves us so — see here His hands, His feet, His side,
  Yes, we know — He is alive.
      Chorus: He is alive!   *(four times)*

6 How lovely on the mountains are the feet of Him
  Who brings good news, good news,
  Announcing peace, proclaiming news of happiness:
  Our God reigns, our God reigns.
      Chorus: Our God reigns!   *(four times)*

117

80 I am the bread of life

S. Suzanne Toolan
Arr. Betty Pulkingham

Rich and full

Capo 3 (G)

1. I am the bread of life; ____ he who comes to me shall not ____
   bread that ____ I will give ____ is my flesh for the life of the
   less ____ you ____ eat ____ of the flesh of the Son of
4. I am the res - ur - rec - tion, I ____ am the ____
   Lord, ____ we be - lieve ____ that ____ you ____ are the ____

hun-ger; he who be-lieves in me shall not thirst. No one can come to
world ____ and he who eats ____ of this bread, he shall ____ live for -
man ____ and ____ drink ____ of his blood, and drink ____ of his
life. ____ He who be-lieves ____ in me, ev - en ____ if he
Christ, ____ the ____ Son ____ of God who ____ has

me ____ un - less the ____ Fa - ther draw him.
ev - er, ____ he shall ____ live for ev - er.
blood ____ you shall not have life with - in you.
die, ____ he shall live for ev - er.
come ____ in - to ____ the ____ world. ____

And I will

raise _____ him up, and I will raise _____ him

up, and I will raise ___ him up ___ on the

1.4

last _____ day.   2. The   day.
3. Un -
5. Yes,

final ending

81 I am trusting Thee

BULLINGER 8 5 8 3

E.W. Bullinger (1837-1913)

1 I am trusting Thee, Lord Jesus,
    Trusting only Thee;
  Trusting Thee for full salvation,
        Great and free.

2 I am trusting Thee for pardon,
    At Thy feet I bow;
  For Thy grace and tender mercy,
        Trusting now.

3 I am trusting Thee for cleansing
    In the crimson flood;
  Trusting Thee to make me holy
        By Thy blood.

4 I am trusting Thee to guide me;
    Thou alone shalt lead,
  Every day and hour supplying
        All my need.

5 I am trusting Thee for power,
    Thine can never fail;
  Words which Thou Thyself shalt give me
        Must prevail.

6 I am trusting Thee, Lord Jesus;
    Never let me fall;
  I am trusting Thee for ever,
        And for all.

Frances Ridley Havergal, 1836-79

82 I am weak but Thou art strong

Traditional arr. Roland Fudge

1 I am weak but Thou art strong;
  Jesus keep me from all wrong
  I'll be satisfied as long
  As I walk, let me walk, close with Thee

Chorus

Just a closer walk with Thee
Grant it, Jesus, this my plea
Daily walking close with Thee
Let it be, dear Lord, let it be.

2 Through this world of toils and snares,
  If I falter, Lord, who cares?
  Who with me my burden shares?
  None but Thee, dear Lord, none but
      Thee.

  Chorus

3 When my feeble life is o'er,
  Time for me will be no more,
  Guide me gently, safely home,
  To Thy Kingdom's shore, to Thy shore.

  Chorus

83   I cannot tell

Irish traditional melody
arranged by Roland Fudge

LONDONDERRY AIR Irregular

1 I cannot tell why He, whom angels worship,
   Should set His love upon the sons of men,
Or why, as Shepherd, He should seek the wanderers,
   To bring them back, they know not how or when.
But this I know, that He was born of Mary,
   When Bethlehem's manger was His only home,
And that He lived at Nazareth and laboured,
   And so the Saviour, Saviour of the world, is come.

2 I cannot tell how silently He suffered,
   As with His peace He graced this place of tears,
Or how His heart upon the Cross was broken,
   The crown of pain to three and thirty years.
But this I know, He heals the broken-hearted,
   And stays our sin, and calms our lurking fear,
And lifts the burden from the heavy laden,
   For yet the Saviour, Saviour of the world, is here.

3 I cannot tell how He will win the nations,
   How He will claim His earthly heritage,
How satisfy the needs and aspirations
   Of East and West, of sinner and of sage.
But this I know, all flesh shall see His glory,
   And He shall reap the harvest He has sown,
And some glad day His sun shall shine in splendour
   When He the Saviour, Saviour of the world, is known.

4 I cannot tell how all the lands shall worship,
   When, at His bidding, every storm is stilled,
Or who can say how great the jubilation
   When all the hearts of men with love are filled.
But this I know, the skies will thrill with rapture,
   And myriad, myriad human voices sing,
And earth to heaven, and heaven to earth, will answer:
   At last the Saviour, Saviour of the world, is King!

William Young Fullerton, 1857-1932

84 I have decided to follow Jesus

Arr. by Cliff Barrows
and Don Hustad

1. I have de - cid - ed___ to fol - low Je - sus,___ I have de -
3. Tho' none go with me,___ I still will fol - low,___ Tho' none go

cid - ed___ to fol - low Je - sus,___ I have de - cid - ed___ to fol - low
with me,___ I still will fol - low, Tho' none go with me,___ I still will

Je - sus,___ No turn-ing back,___ no turn-ing back.___ 2. The world be -
fol - low,___ No turn-ing back,___ no turn-ing back.___ 4. Will you de -

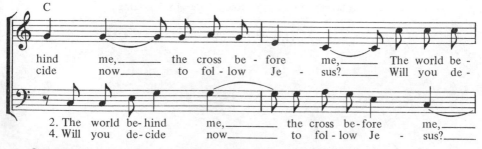

hind me,___ the cross be - fore me,___ The world be -
cide now___ to fol - low Je - sus?___ Will you de -

2. The world be- hind me,___ the cross be - fore me,___
4. Will you de - cide now___ to fol - low Je - sus?___

hind me,_____ the cross be - fore me,_____ The world be-
cide now_____ to fol - low Je - sus?_____ Will you de-

_ The world be-hind me,_____ the cross be-fore me,_____
_ Will you de-cide now_____ to fol - low Je - sus?_____

hind me,_____ the cross be - fore me,_____ No turn-ing
cide now_____ to fol - low Je - sus?_____ No turn-ing

_ The world be-hind me,_____ the cross be-fore me,_____
_ Will you de-cide now_____ to fol - low Je - sus?_____

Am Dm G   C
Coda

G   C   D.C.

back,_____ no turn-ing back._____ No turn-ing back!_____
back,_____ no turn-ing back._____ No turn-ing back!

_ No turn-ing back, no turn-ing back._____
_ No turn-ing back, no turn-ing back._____

85(i)　I heard the voice of Jesus say

VOX DILECTI

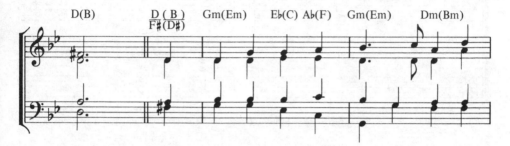

85(ii)

KINGSFOLD

arr. & harm. Ralph Vaughan Williams (1872–1958)

1 I heard the voice of Jesus say:
   Come unto Me and rest;
Lay down, thou weary one, lay down
   Thy head upon My breast!
I came to Jesus as I was,
   Weary, and worn, and sad;
I found in Him a resting-place,
   And He has made me glad.

2 I heard the voice of Jesus say:
   Behold, I freely give
The living water; thirsty one,
   Stoop down and drink, and live!
I came to Jesus, and I drank
   Of that life-giving stream;
My thirst was quenched, my soul revived,
   And now I live in Him.

3 I heard the voice of Jesus say:
   I am this dark world's Light;
Look unto Me, thy morn shall rise,
   And all thy day be bright!
I looked to Jesus, and I found
   In Him my star, my sun;
And in that light of life I'll walk
   Till travelling days are done.

Horatius Bonar, 1808-89

From the *English Hymnal* by permission of Oxford University Press.

86(i) I know that my Redeemer lives

CHURCH TRIUMPHANT 8 8 8 8 (L.M.) J.W. Elliot (1883-1915)

1 I know that my Redeemer lives!
  What joy the blest assurance gives!
  He lives, He lives, who once was dead;
  He lives, my everlasting Head!

2 He lives, to bless me with His love;
  He lives, to plead for me above;
  He lives, my hungry soul to feed;
  He lives, to help in time of need.

3 He lives, and grants me daily breath;
  He lives, and I shall conquer death;
  He lives, my mansion to prepare;
  He lives, to lead me safely there.

4 He lives, all glory to His name;
  He lives, my Saviour, still the same;
  What joy the blest assurance gives!
  I know that my Redeemer lives!

Samuel Medley, 1738-99

128

86(ii)

PHILIPPINE L.M.

R.E. Roberts (1878-1940)

1 I know that my Redeemer lives!
What joy the blest assurance gives!
He lives, He lives, who once was dead;
He lives, my everlasting Head!

2 He lives, to bless me with His love;
He lives, to plead for me above;
He lives, my hungry soul to feed;
He lives, to help in time of need.

3 He lives, and grants me daily breath;
He lives, and I shall conquer death;
He lives, my mansion to prepare;
He lives, to lead me safely there.

4 He lives, all glory to His name;
He lives, my Saviour, still the same;
What joy the blest assurance gives!;
I know that my Redeemer lives!

Samuel Medley, 1738-99

87　I love you Lord

Laurie Klein

With feeling

I love You, Lord,_____ and I lift my voice_____

_____ To wor - ship You, O my

soul re - joice. Take joy, my King,_____

_____ in_____ what You hear,_____ May it be a

sweet, sweet__ sound in__ Your ear._____

88 I hear the sound of rustling

With pace

R. Wilson

1. I hear the sound of rust-ling in the leaves of the trees, The Spi-rit of the Lord has come down on the earth. The Church that seemed in slum-ber has now ris-en from its knees And dry bones are res-pond-ing with the fruits of new birth. Oh

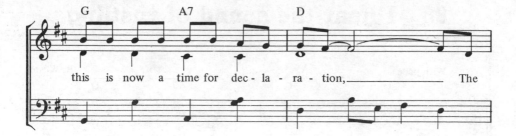

this is now a time for dec - la - ra - tion,_____ The

word will go to all men ev - 'ry - where,_____ The

Church is here for heal - ing of the na - tions,_____ Be -

hold the day of Je - sus draw - ing near._____ My

tongue will be the pen of a rea - dy wri - ter,_____ And

what the Fa-ther gives to me I'll sing,_____ I

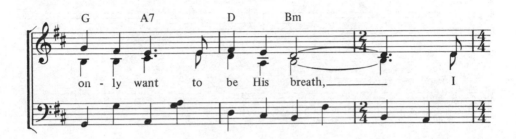

on - ly want to be His breath,_____ I

on - ly want to glo - ri - fy the King._____

2 And all around the world the body waits expectantly,
The promise of the Father is now ready to fall.
The watchmen on the tower all exhort us to prepare
And the church responds — a people who will answer the call.
And this is not a phase which is passing,
It's the start of an age that is to come.
And where is the wise man and the scoffer?
Before the face of Jesus they are dumb.

3 A body now prepared by God and ready for war,
The prompting of the Spirit is our word of command.
We rise, a mighty army, at the bidding of the Lord,
The devils see and fear, for their time is at hand.
And children of the Lord hear our commission
That we should love and serve our God as one.
The Spirit won't be hindered by division
In the perfect work that Jesus has begun.

89 I know whom I have believed

James McGranahan (1840-1907)

1 I know not why God's wondrous grace
    To me has been made known;
Nor why — unworthy as I am
    He claimed me for His own.

    But "I know whom I have believed
    and am persuaded that He is able to
    keep that which I've committed unto
    Him against that day."

2 I know not how this saving faith
    To me He did impart;
Or how believing in His word
    Wrought peace within my heart.

    But "I know. . . . "

3 I know not how the Spirit moves,
    Convincing men of sin;
Revealing Jesus through the word,
    Creating faith in Him.

    But "I know. . . . "

4 I know not what of good or ill
    May be reserved for me —
Of weary ways or golden days
    Before His face I see.

    But "I know. . . . "

    D.W. Whittle, 1840-1901

90   I love my Lord

David G. Wilson

1 I love my Lord because He heard my voice.
My God, He listens to my prayer.
Because He hears me when I call on Him,
Through all my days I shall pray.

2 My soul was saved from death; my eyes from tears;
My feet now walk before the Lord;
Yet in despair I thought my end was near
My faith in life disappeared.

3 What can I do to thank God for His love—
For all His benefits to me?
I will lift up salvation's cup on high
And call on Him by His Name.

4 My vows to Him I promise to fulfil,
To Him I sacrifice my life.
He freed me from the servitude of sin
And now I serve as His slave.

5 Unite in praise, great family of God,
His children, bring to Him your thanks.
City of peace, where God has made His home
With one accord, praise His Name!

© J.M. Barnes

91 I love the name of Jesus

Capo 3 (D)

Tenderly

Kathleen Thomerson

1. I love the name of Je - sus, King of my heart, he is
2. I love the name of Je - sus, ri - sen a - bove, and he
3. I love the name of Je - sus, splen - dour of God, and his

ev - 'ry - thing to me. I bless the name of Je - sus,
loves and prays for me. I bless the name of Je - sus,
face I long to see. I bless the name of Je - sus,

reign in my life, show the Fa - ther's love so free.
rul - ing on high with a glo - rious ma - jes - ty.
shep - herd of men; by his side I now can be.

Spi - rit of love, spi - rit of power, shine through e - ter - ni -

I love the name of Je - sus,
I praise the name of Je - sus,
I praise the name of Je - sus,

light of the world, let me walk each day with thee.
Lord of my life, for he died to set me free.
for he is love, and that love he gives to me.

92 I need thee every hour

I NEED THEE

R. Lowry (1826-99)

1. I need Thee ev-'ry hour, Most gra - cious Lord;
2. I need Thee ev-'ry hour, Stay Thou near by;
3. I need Thee ev-'ry hour, In joy or pain;

No ten - der voice like Thine Can peace af - ford.
Temp - ta - tions lose their pow'r When Thou art nigh.
Come quick - ly and a - bide Or life is vain.

REFRAIN

I need Thee, O I need Thee! Ev - 'ry hour I need Thee:

O bless me now, my Sav - iour! I come to Thee.

4 I need Thee every hour,
   Teach me Thy will;
   And Thy rich promises
   In me fulfil.

5 I need Thee every hour,
   Most Holy One;
   O make me Thine indeed,
   Thou blessèd Son!

Annie Sherwood Hawks (1835-1918)

93 I want to worship the Lord

Composer unknown
Arr. Roland Fudge

With quiet adoration

I want to wor - ship the Lord with all of my

heart, give him my all and not just a

part. lift up my hands to the King of

Kings, praise him in ev - ery - thing.

94 I serve a risen Saviour

(He lives!)

A.H.A.
Capo 3

A.H. Ackley

1. I serve a ris - en Sav - iour, He's in the world to -
2. In all the world a - round me I see His lov - ing
3. Re - joice, re - joice, O Chris - tian, lift up your voice and

day;____ I know that He is liv - ing, what -
care,____ And tho' my heart grows wea - ry I
sing____ E - ter - nal hal - le - lu - jahs to

ev - er men may say;____ I see His hand of
nev - er will de - spair;____ I know that He is
Je - sus Christ the King!____ The Hope of all who

mer - cy, I hear His voice of cheer.____ And
lead - ing, thro' all the storm - y blast,____ The
seek Him, the Help of all who find,____ None

just the time I need Him____ He's al - ways near.____
day of His ap - pear-ing____ will come at last.____
oth - er is so lov-ing,____ so good and kind.____

REFRAIN

He lives,____ He lives,____ Christ Je-sus lives to - day!____ He
He lives, He lives,

walks with me and talks with me a - long life's nar - row way.____ He

lives,____ He lives,____ sal - va - tion to im - part!____ You
He lives, He lives,

ask me how I know He lives? He lives with-in my heart.____

143

95   I trust in Thee O Lord

M. Warrington
Arr. Jeanne Harper

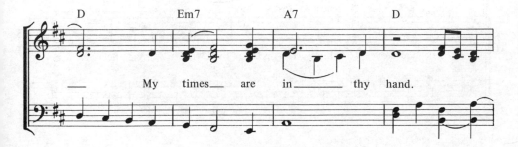

Bless - ed be___ the Lord,___

___ for he has won-drous - ly shown___

___ his stead - fast love___ to me,___

___ his stead - fast love to me.___

96 I will call upon the Lord

Rich Cook

97 I will enter His gates

98 I will give thanks

Brent Chambers
arr. Roland Fudge

Rich and unhurried

I will give thanks to Thee, O Lord, a-mong the peo- ples. I will sing prais- es to Thee a-mong the na- tions. For Thy stead - fast love is, great, is great to the heav - ens, and Thy faith - ful-ness, Thy faith-ful-ness, to the clouds.

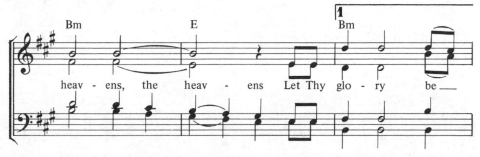

99 I will sing, I will sing

Liltingly

Max Dyer

I will sing, I will sing a song— un-to the Lord. I will
Chorus Al - le - lu, al - le - lu - ia, glo - ry to the Lord. Al - le -

sing, I will sing a song— un-to the Lord. I will sing, I will sing a song
lu, al-le-lu - ia, glo - ry to the Lord. Al-le-lu, al-le-lu - ia, glo -

Repeat for Chorus

— un-to the Lord. Al-le - lu - ia, glo - ry to the Lord.
ry to the Lord. Al-le - lu - ia, glo - ry to the Lord.

Optional verses:

> We will come, we will come as one before the Lord.
> Alleluia, glory to the Lord.

> If the Son, if the Son shall make you free,
> You shall be free indeed.

> They that sow in tears shall reap in joy.
> Alleluia, glory to the Lord.

> Ev'ry knee shall bow and ev'ry tongue confess
> That Jesus Christ is Lord.

> In his name, in his name we have the victory.
> Alleluia, glory to the Lord.

Most effective sung unaccompanied, but with
light clapping. Suggested rhythm:　etc.

100 I'm not ashamed to own my Lord

JACKSON   Thomas Jackson (1715-81)

1. I'm not a-shamed to own my Lord, Or to de-fend His cause, Main-tain the hon-our of His Word, The glo-ry of His cross.

2. Je-sus, my God! I know His name, His Name is all my trust; Nor will He put my soul to shame, Nor let my hope be lost.

3. Firm as His throne His pro-mise stands, And He can well se-cure What I've com-mit-ted to His hands, Till the de-ci-sive hour.

4 Then will He own my worthless name
  Before His Father's face;
  And, in the New Jerusalem,
  Appoint my soul a place.

Isaac Watts 1674-1748

151

101   I will sing the wondrous story

HYFRYDOL 8 7. 8 7. D

Melody by R.H. Prichard, 1811-87

1 I will sing the wondrous story
    Of the Christ who died for me, —
How He left the realms of glory
    For the cross on Calvary.
Yes, I'll sing the wondrous story
    Of the Christ who died for me, —
Sing it with His saints in glory,
    Gathered by the crystal sea.

2 I was lost: but Jesus found me,
    Found the sheep that went astray,
Raised me up and gently led me
    Back into the narrow way.
Days of darkness still may meet me,
    Sorrow's paths I oft may tread;
But His presence still is with me,
    By His guiding hand I'm led.

3 He will keep me till the river
    Rolls its waters at my feet:
Then He'll bear me safely over,
    Made by grace for glory meet.
Yes, I'll sing the wondrous story
    Of the Christ who died for me, —
Sing it with His saints in glory,
    Gathered by the crystal sea.

F.H. Rawley, 1854-1952

102   I will sing unto the Lord

Donya Brockway
arranged Margaret Evans

Easy waltz feel

I will sing un-to the Lord as long as I live,

I will sing praise to my God while I have my be-ing,____

____ My me-di-ta-tion of Him

shall_ be sweet, I will be glad I will be glad in the

Lord._____ Bless thou the Lord, O my soul,

Praise ye the Lord._____ Bless thou the Lord, O my

soul, Praise ye the Lord._____ Bless thou the Lord,

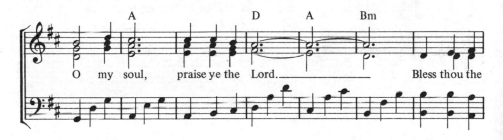

O my soul, praise ye the Lord._____ Bless thou the

Lord, O my soul, praise ye the Lord._____

103 Immortal, invisible

ST. DENIO 11 11 11 11

Welsh hymn melody (1839)

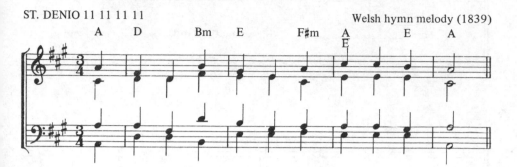

1 Immortal, invisible, God only wise,
  In light inaccessible hid from our eyes,
  Most blessèd, most glorious, the Ancient of Days,
  Almighty, victorious, Thy great name we praise.

2 Unresting, unhasting, and silent as light,
  Nor wanting, nor wasting, Thou rulest in might;
  Thy justice like mountains high soaring above,
  Thy clouds which are fountains of goodness and love.

3 To all life Thou givest — to both great and small;
  In all life Thou livest, the true life of all;
  We blossom and flourish as leaves on the tree,
  And wither and perish — but nought changeth Thee.

4 Great Father of Glory, pure Father of Light,
  Thine angels adore Thee, all veiling their sight;
  All laud we would render; O help us to see:
  'Tis only the splendour of light hideth Thee.

5 Immortal, invisible, God only wise,
  In light inaccessible hid from our eyes,
  Most blessèd, most glorious, the Ancient of Days,
  Almighty, victorious, Thy great name we praise.

Walter Chalmers Smith, 1824-1908

104　In full and glad surrender

Frances Ridley Havergal (1836-79)

Henry John Gauntlett

ST. ALPHEGE

1. In full and glad sur - ren - der I
2. O Son of God, Who lov'st me, I
3. Reign ov - er me, Lord Je - sus; O
4. O come and reign, Lord Je - sus; Rule

give my - self to Thee, Thine ut - ter - ly and
will be Thine a - lone; And all I have and
make my heart Thy throne; It shall be Thine, dear
ov - er ev - ery - thing! And keep me al - ways

on - ly And ev - er - more to be.
am, Lord, Shall hence - forth be Thine own!
Sav - iour, It shall be Thine a - lone.
loy - al, And true to Thee, my King.

105 / In my life Lord, be glorified

Bob Kilpatrick
arr. R. Fudge

With devotion

In my life Lord, Lord,

be glo-ri-fied, be glo-ri-fied; in my

life Lord, be glo-ri-fied to-day.

2 In your church, Lord, be glorified, be glorified;
In your church, Lord, be glorified today.

106 In heavenly love abiding

PENLAN 7 6 7 6 D

D. Jenkins (1849-1915)

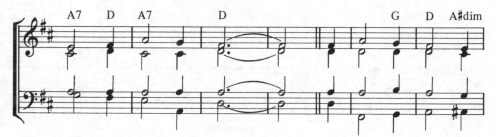

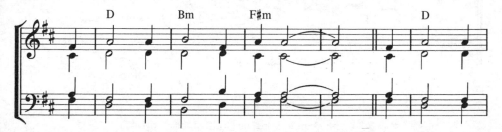

1 In heavenly love abiding,
    No change my heart shall fear;
And safe is such confiding,
    For nothing changes here:
The storm may roar without me,
    My heart may low be laid;
But God is round about me,
    And can I be dismayed?

2 Wherever He may guide me,
    No want shall turn me back;
My Shepherd is beside me,
    And nothing can I lack:
His wisdom ever waketh,
    His sight is never dim;
He knows the way He taketh,
    And I will walk with Him.

3 Green pastures are before me,
    Which yet I have not seen;
Bright skies will soon be o'er me,
    Where the dark clouds have been:
My hope I cannot measure,
    My path to life is free;
My Saviour has my treasure,
    And He will walk with me.

Anna Laetitia Waring 1820-1910

107 In the cross of Christ I glory

ST. OSWALD 8 7. 8 7

J.B. Dykes, (1823-76)

1 In the cross of Christ I glory,
    Towering o'er the wrecks of time;
All the light of sacred story
    Gathers round its head sublime,

2 When the woes of life o'ertake me,
    Hopes deceive, and fears annoy,
Never shall the cross forsake me;
    Lo! it glows with peace and joy.

3 When the sun of bliss is beaming
    Light and love upon my way,
From the cross the radiance streaming
    Adds more lustre to the day.

4 Bane and blessing, pain and pleasure,
    By the cross are sanctified;
Peace is there that knows no measure,
    Joys that through all time abide.

5 In the cross of Christ I glory,
    Towering o'er the wrecks of time:
All the light of sacred story
    Gathers round its head sublime.

John Bowring, 1792-1872

108   In the presence of your people

Psalm 22:3, 25

Brent Chambers

In the pre-sence of your peo-ple I will praise your name

for a-lone you are ho-ly, en-throned on the prais-es of Is-ra-el.

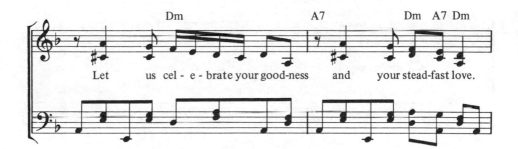

Let us cel-e-brate your good-ness and your stead-fast love.

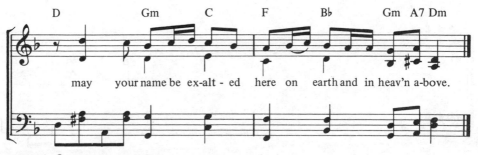

may your name be ex-alt-ed here on earth and in heav'n a-bove.

109   In the name of Jesus

Composer unknown
arr. Roland Fudge

Arr. Copyright © 1983 Roland Fudge.

164

Who can tell what God can do?

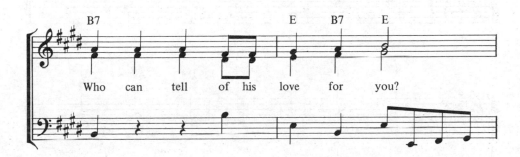

Who can tell of his love for you?

In the name of Je - sus, Je - sus,

we have the vic - to - ry.

110 It is a thing most wonderful

BROOKFIELD

T.B. Southgate (1814-68)

1 It is a thing most wonderful,
   Almost too wonderful to be,
That God's own Son should come from heaven,
   And die to save a child like me.

2 And yet I know that it is true;
   He chose a poor and humble lot,
And wept and toiled and mourned and died,
   For love of those who loved Him not.

3 I sometimes think about the Cross,
   And shut my eyes and try to see
The cruel nails and crown of thorns,
   And Jesus crucified for me.

4 But even could I see Him die,
   I could but see a little part
Of that great love which like a fire
   Is always burning in His heart.

5 I cannot tell how He could love
   A child so weak and full of sin;
His love must be most wonderful,
   If He could die my love to win.

6 It is most wonderful to know
   His love for me so free and sure;
But 'tis more wonderful to see
   My love for Him so faint and poor.

7 And yet I want to love Thee, Lord;
   O light the flame within my heart,
And I will love Thee more and more,
   Until I see Thee as Thou art.

William Walsham How 1823-97

111 It only takes a spark

PASS IT ON

Kurt Kaiser

1. It___ on - ly takes a spark to get a fire___
2. What a won - drous time is spring when all the trees are
3. I___ wish for you, my friend, this hap - pi - ness that

go - ing___ And soon all those a - round can
bud - ding___ The birds be - gin to sing; The
I've___ found___ You can de - pend on Him, It

warm up in its glow - ing___ That's how it is with
flow - ers start their bloom - ing___ That's how it is with
mat - ters not where you're bound___ I'll shout it from the

God's love Once you've ex - per - i - enced it___ you
God's love Once you've ex - per - i - enced it___ you
mountain top, I want my world to know;___ The

spread His love to ev - ery - one; You want to pass it on.___
want to sing, it's fresh like spring; You want to pass it on.___
Lord of love has come to me, I want to pass it on.___

112 It passeth knowledge

10 10. 10 10. 4

I.D. Sankey (1840-1908)

1 It passeth knowledge, that dear love of
    Thine,
  My Saviour, Jesus! Yet this soul of
    mine
  Would of Thy love, in all its breadth
    and length,
  Its height and depth, and everlasting
    strength,
    Know more and more.

2 It passeth telling, that dear love of
    Thine,
  My Saviour, Jesus! Yet these lips of
    mine
  Would fain proclaim to sinners far and
    near
  A love which can remove all guilty
    fear,
    And love beget.

3 It passeth praises, that dear love of
    Thine,
  My Saviour, Jesus! Yet this heart of
    mine

Would sing that love, so full, so rich,
    so free,
Which brings a rebel sinner, such as me,
    Nigh unto God.

4 O fill me, Saviour, Jesus, with Thy
    love!
  Lead, lead me to the living fount above;
  Thither may I, in simple faith, draw
    nigh,
  And never to another fountain fly,
    But unto Thee.

5 And then, when Jesus face to face I see,
  When at His lofty throne I bow the
    knee,
  Then of His love, in all its breadth and
    length,
  Its height and depth, its everlasting
    strength,
    My soul shall sing.

Mary Shekleton, 1827-83

169

113 I've found a friend

CONSTANCE 8.7.8.7.D. Iambic

A. Sullivan (1842-1900)

1 I've found a friend; O such a friend!
      He loved me ere I knew Him;
   He drew me with the cords of love,
      And thus He bound me to Him;
   And round my heart still closely twine
      Those ties which nought can sever;
   For I am His, and He is mine,
      For ever and for ever.

2 I've found a friend; O such a Friend!
      He bled, He died to save me;
   And not alone the gift of life,
      But His own self He gave me.
   Nought that I have mine own I call,
      I hold it for the Giver:
   My heart, my strength, my life, my all
      Are His, and His for ever.

3 I've found a Friend; O such a Friend!
      All power to Him is given,
   To guard me on my onward course
      And bring me safe to heaven.
   Eternal glories gleam afar,
      To nerve my faint endeavour;
   So now to watch, to work, to war,
      And then to rest for ever.

4 I've found a Friend; O such a Friend,
      So kind, and true, and tender!
   So wise a Counsellor and Guide,
      So mighty a Defender!
   From Him who loves me now so well
      What power my soul shall sever?
   Shall life or death? shall earth or hell?
      No! I am His for ever.

James Grindlay Small 1817-88

114 I've got peace like a river

Traditional
arr. Roland Fudge

Quietly

I've got peace like a ri - ver, peace like a

ri - ver, I've got peace like a ri - ver in my soul,

I've got peace like a ri - ver, peace like a

ri - ver, I've got peace like a ri - ver in my soul.

Alternative version:
Lively

I've got peace like a ri - ver, I've got peace like a
ri - ver, I've got peace like a ri - ver in my *(etc.)*

115 Jesus, Lamb of God

From *'Mass for the King of Glory'*

Slow and sustained

Betty Pulkingham

Je - sus, Lamb of God, have mer - cy on us. Je - sus, bear - er of our sins, have mer - cy on us. Je - sus, re - deem - er of the world, give us your peace.

1 Give us your peace. **2**

116 Jesus calls us, o'er the tumult

ST. ANDREW 87.87

E.H. Thorne (1834-1916)

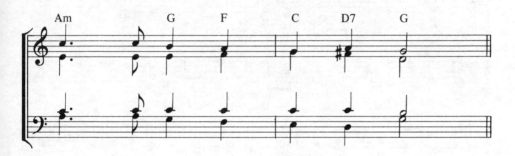

1 Jesus calls us; o'er the tumult
    Of our life's wild restless sea,
  Day by day His voice is sounding,
    Saying, "Christian, follow me";

2 As, of old, apostles heard it
    By the Galilean lake,
  Turned from home, and toil, and kindred,
    Leaving all for His dear sake.

3 Jesus calls us from the worship
    Of the vain world's golden store,
  From each idol that would keep us,
    Saying, "Christian, love Me more."

4 In our joys and in our sorrows,
    Days of toil and hours of ease,
  Still He calls, in cares and pleasures,
    "Christian, love Me more than these."

5 Jesus calls us! By Thy mercies,
    Saviour, may we hear Thy call,
  Give our hearts to Thine obedience,
    Serve and love Thee best of all.

Cecil Frances Alexander, 1818-95

117 Jesus Christ is alive today

Composer unknown
arr. Roland Fudge

Joyfully

Je - sus Christ is a - live to - day, I we}

know I we} know it's true.

Sov' - reign of the U - ni - verse, I we}

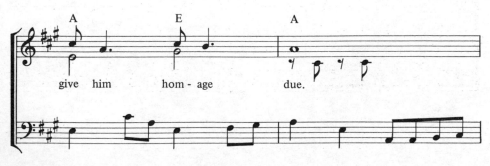

give him hom - age due.

Seat - ed there at God's right hand,

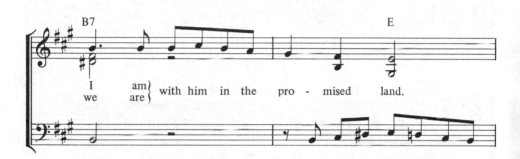

I am } with him in the pro - mised land.
we are }

Je - sus lives and reigns in { me, that's
{ you,

how I know it's true.

118　Jesus, how lovely You are

David Bolton

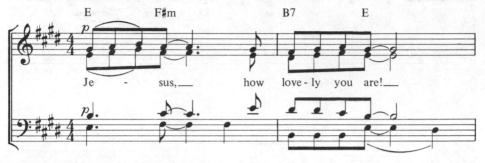

Je - sus,___ how love - ly you are!___

You are so gen - tle so pure___ and kind,___

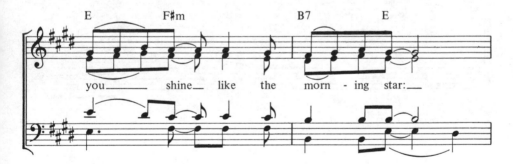

you___ shine___ like the morn - ing star:___

Fine

Je - sus___ how love - ly you are.

Al - le - lu - ia, Je - sus is my Lord (my and

Lord and king) Al - le - lu - ia, Je - sus is
king

(my eve - ry - thing. ry - thing.)
my

2 Alleluia, Jesus died and rose again;
   alleluia, Jesus forgave all my sin.
   Jesus, how lovely you are . . !

3 Alleluia, Jesus is meek and lowly;
   alleluia, Jesus is pure and holy.
   Jesus how lovely you are . . !

4 Alleluia, Jesus is the bridegroom;
   alleluia, Jesus will take his bride soon.
   Jesus how lovely you are . . !

119 Jesus is Lord

David J. Mansell

1. Je-sus is Lord! Cre - a - tion's voice pro-claims it,
2. Je-sus is Lord! Yet from his throne e - ter - nal
3. Je-sus is Lord! O'er sin the might-y con - queror,

For by his power each tree and flower was planned and made.
In flesh he came to die in pain on Calv'-ry's tree.
From death he rose and all his foes shall own his name.

Je-sus is Lord! The u - ni-verse de - clares it.
Je-sus is Lord! From him all life pro-ceed - ing,
Je-sus is Lord! God sends his Ho-ly Spi - rit

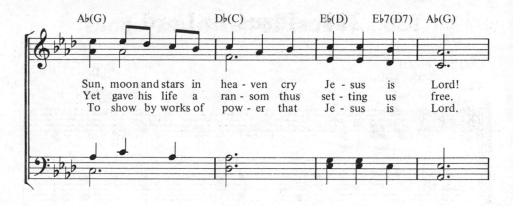

Sun, moon and stars in hea - ven cry Je - sus is Lord!
Yet gave his life a ran - som thus set - ting us free.
To show by works of pow - er that Je - sus is Lord.

REFRAIN

Je - sus is Lord! Je - sus is Lord!

Praise him with 'Hal - le - lu - jahs' for Je - sus is Lord!

120   Jesus, lover of my soul

ABERYSTWYTH 77.77.D

Joseph Parry (1841-1903)

1 Jesus, lover of my soul,
    Let me to Thy bosom fly,
While the nearer waters roll,
    While the tempest still is high:
Hide me, O my Saviour, hide,
    Till the storm of life is past;
Safe into the haven guide;
    O receive my soul at last!

2 Other refuge have I none,
    Hangs my helpless soul on Thee;
Leave, ah! leave me not alone,
    Still support and comfort me:
All my trust on Thee is stayed;
    All my help from Thee I bring;
Cover my defenceless head
    With the shadow of Thy wing.

3 Thou, O Christ, art all I want;
    More than all in Thee I find;
Raise the fallen, cheer the faint,
    Heal the sick, and lead the blind.
Just and holy is Thy name,
    I am all unrighteousness;
False, and full of sin I am,
    Thou art full of truth and grace.

4 Plenteous grace with Thee is found,
    Grace to cover all my sin;
Let the healing streams abound,
    Make and keep me pure within.
Thou of life the fountain art,
    Freely let me take of Thee;
Spring Thou up within my heart,
    Rise to all eternity.

Charles Wesley 1707-88 , altd.

121 Jesus my Lord
(Now I belong to Jesus)

N.J. Clayton

N.J. Clayton

Capo 1

1. Je-sus my Lord will love me for ev-er, From Him no pow'r of ev-il can se-ver He gave His life to ran-som my soul, Now I be-long to Him:

CHORUS

Now I be-long to Je-sus, Je-sus be-longs to me, Not for the years of time a-lone, But for e-ter-ni-ty.

2 Once I was lost in sin's degradation,
Jesus came down to bring me salvation,
Lifted me up from sorrow and shame,
Now I belong to Him:

Chorus

3 Joy floods my soul for Jesus has saved
   me,
Freed me from sin that long had
   enslaved me,
His precious blood He gave to redeem,
Now I belong to Him:

Chorus

122 Jesus, name above all names

Nada Hearn
arr. Roland Fudge

Slow and gentle

Je - sus,_____ Name a-bove all names,_____ Beau - ti-ful

sav - iour,_____ glor - i - ous Lord,_____ Em -

man - u - el,_____ God is with us,_____ Bless - ed Re-

deem - er_____ Liv - ing Word._____

123 Jesus shall reign

TRURO 8 8 8 8 (L.M.)   Psalmodia Evangelica 1789

1 Jesus shall reign where'er the sun
Does his successive journeys run;
His kingdom stretch from shore to shore
Till moons shall rise and set no more.

2 To him shall endless prayer be made,
And princes throng to crown his head;
His name like sweet perfume shall rise
With every morning sacrifice.

3 People and realms of every tongue
Dwell on his love with sweetest song;
And infant voices shall proclaim
Their early blessings on his name.

4 Blessings abound where'er he reigns;
The prisoner leaps to lose his chains,
The weary find eternal rest,
And all the sons of want are bless'd.

5 Let every creature rise and bring
The highest honours to our King;
Angels descend with songs again;
And earth repeat the loud Amen.

Isaac Watts, 1674-1748

186

124 Jesus stand among us

With warmth

G. Kendrick

1. Je-sus, stand a-mong us at the meet-ing of our lives,

Be our sweet a-gree-ment at the meet-ing of our eyes; O,

Je-sus, we love You so we ga-ther here,

Join our hearts in un-i-ty and take a-way our

fear. our fear.

2 So to You we're gathering out of each and every land,
Christ the love between us at the joining of our hands;
O, Jesus, we love You, so we gather here,
Join our hearts in unity and take away our fear.

125 Jesus, stand among us in Thy risen power

CASWALL 6.5.6.5

F. Filitz (1804-76)

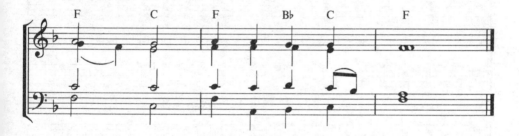

1 Jesus, stand among us
   In Thy risen power;
Let this time of worship
   Be a hallowed hour.

2 Breathe the Holy Spirit
   Into every heart;
Bid the fears and sorrows
   From each soul depart.

3 Thus with quickened footsteps
   We'll pursue our way,
Watching for the dawning
   Of eternal day.

William Pennefather 1816-73

126 Jesus! The name high over all

LYDIA
Charles Wesley
Capo 1 (D)

Thomas Phillips

1. Je - sus, the name high o - ver all,
In hell, or earth, or sky: An - gels and men be - fore it fall, And de - vils fear and fly. And de - vils fear and fly.

2. Je - sus, the name to sin - ners dear,
The name to sin - ners giv'n; I scat - ters all their guil - ty fear, It turns their hell to heav'n. It turns their hell to heav'n.

3. Je - sus the pris - on - er's fet - ters breaks,
And bruis - es Sa - tan's head; Pow'r in - to strength-less souls He speaks, And life in - to the dead. And life in - to the dead.

4. Oh, that the world might taste and see.
The rich - es of His grace! The arms of love that com - pass me, Would all man - kind em - brace. Would all man - kind em - brace.

5. His on - ly right - eous - ness I show,
His sav - ing truth pro - claim: 'Tis all my busi - ness here be - low, To cry Be - hold the Lamb! To cry Be - hold the Lamb.

6. Hap - py, if with my lat - est breath
I may but gasp His name: Preach Him to all and cry in death, "Be - hold, be - hold the Lamb!" "Be - hold, be - hold the Lamb."

189

127 Jesus take me as I am

Tenderly

Capo 4 (C)

D. Bryant

Je-sus take me as I am,

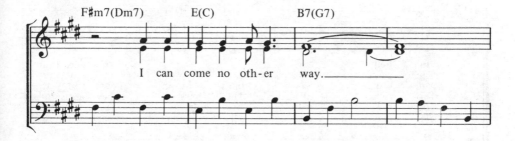

I can come no oth-er way.

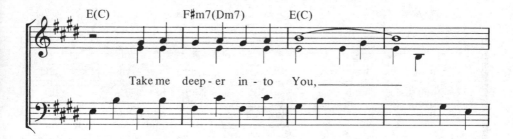

Take me deep-er in-to You,

Make my flesh life melt a - way.

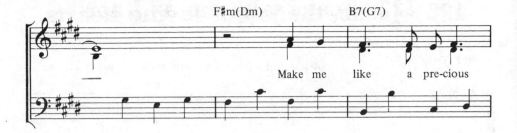

Make me   like   a pre-cious

stone,_____   Crys-tal

clear   and fine - ly   honed._____

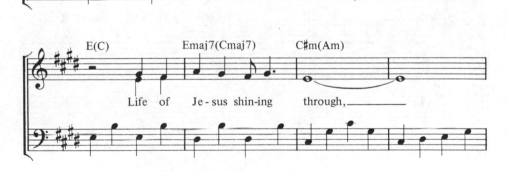

Life   of   Je - sus shin-ing   through,_____

Giv-ing   glo - ry   back to   You._____

128 Jesus, the joy of loving hearts

MARYTON 8 8 8 8 (LM)

H.P. Smith (1825-98)

Capo 1 (D)

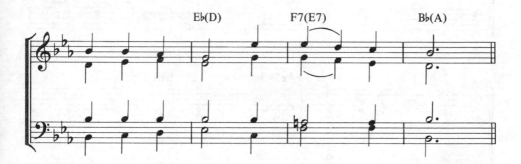

1 Jesus, the joy of loving hearts,
   True source of life, and light of men:
   From the best bliss that earth imparts
   We turn unfilled to you again.

2 Your truth unchanged has ever stood,
   You rescue those who on you call;
   To those yet seeking, you are good —
   To those who find you, all-in-all.

3 We taste of you, the living bread,
   And long to feast upon you still;
   We drink from you, the fountain-head,
   Our thirsty souls from you we fill.

4 Our restless spirits long for you,
   Whichever way our lot is cast,
   Glad when your gracious smile we view,
   Blessed when our faith can hold you fast.

5 Jesus, for ever with us stay,
   Make all our moments calm and bright;
   Chase the dark night of sin away,
   Spread through the world your holy light.

from the Latin (twelfth century)
R. Palmer 1808-87

129 Jesus the very thought of Thee

Bernard of Clairvaux 1091–1153
Tr. by Edward Caswall 1814–78

John B. Dykes

1. Je - sus, the ve - ry thought of Thee
2. Nor voice can sing, nor heart can frame,
3. O Hope of ev - 'ry con - trite heart,
4. But what to those who find? Ah, this
5. Je - sus, our on - ly joy be Thou,

With sweet - ness fills the breast;
Nor can the mem - 'ry find
O Joy of all the meek,
Nor tongue nor pen can show:
As Thou our prize wilt be;

But sweet - er far Thy face to see,
A sweet - er sound than Thy blest name,
To those who ask, how kind Thou art!
The love of Je - sus, what it is,
In Thee be all our glo - ry now,

And in Thy pres - ence rest.
O Sav - iour of man - kind!
How good to those who seek!
None but His loved ones know.
And thro' e - ter - ni - ty.

130 Jubilate Deo

PSALM 100
Capo 5 (Am)

With vigour

F. Dunn

Ju - bi -la - te, ev - 'ry-bo - dy, serve the Lord in all your ways, and come be-fore his pre - sence sing-ing; en - ter now his courts with praise. For the Lord our God is gra - cious, and his mer - cy ev - er- last - ing. Ju - bi - la - te, ju - bi - 'te, ju - bi - la - te De - o!

131 Jesus we enthrone You

P. Kyle
arr. R. Fudge

With adoration

Je - sus___ we en - throne___ You___

___ We pro - claim You our King.

Stand-ing here___ in the midst of us___

We raise You up___ with our praise,___

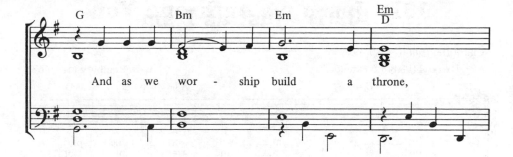

And as we wor - ship build a throne,

And as we wor - ship build a throne

And as we wor - ship build a throne. Come Lord

Je - sus and take___ Your place.___

132(i) Just as I am

Charlotte Elliott 1789–1871

WOODWORTH 8 8 8 6 extended

W.B. Bradbury (1816-68)

1. Just as I am, without one plea,
   But that Thy blood was shed for me,
   And that Thou bidd'st me come to Thee,
   O Lamb of God, I come! I come!

2. Just as I am, and waiting not
   To rid my soul of one dark blot,
   To Thee, whose blood can cleanse each spot,
   O Lamb of God, I come! I come!

3. Just as I am, tho' tossed about
   With many a conflict, many a doubt,
   Fightings within, and fears without,
   O Lamb of God, I come! I come!

4. Just as I am, poor, wretched, blind,
   Sight, riches, healing of the mind,
   Yea, all I need, in Thee to find,
   O Lamb of God, I come! I come!

5. Just as I am, Thou wilt receive,
   Wilt welcome, pardon, cleanse, relieve;
   Because Thy promise I believe,
   O Lamb of God, I come! I come!

6. Just as I am, Thy love unknown
   Hath broken ev'ry barrier down;
   Now, to be Thine, yea, Thine alone,
   O Lamb of God, I come! I come!

132(ii)

MISERICORDIA 8 8 8 6

Henry Smart (1813-79)

1. Just as I am, with-out one plea,
2. Just as I am, and wait - ing not
3. Just as I am, tho' tossed a - bout,
4. Just as I am, poor, wretch - ed, blind,
5. Just as I am, Thou wilt re - ceive,
6. Just as I am, Thy love un - known

But that Thy blood was shed for me,
To rid my soul of one dark blot,
With many a con - flict, many a doubt,
Sight, rich - es heal - ing of the mind,
Wilt wel - come, par - don, cleanse, re - lieve;
Hath bro - ken ev - 'ry bar - rier down;

And that Thou bidd'st me come to Thee,
To Thee, whose blood can cleanse each spot,
Fight - ings with - in, and fears with - out,
Yea, all I need, in Thee to find,
Be - cause Thy pro - mise I be - lieve,
Now, to be Thine, yea, Thine a - lone,

O

Lamb of God, I come.

133 Let all that is within me

Anon.
Arr. Betty Pulkingham

Let all that is with-in me____ cry, 'Ho-ly.'____

____ Let all that is with-in me____ cry,

'Ho-ly.'____ Ho-ly,

Ho-ly, Ho-ly is the Lamb that was slain.

Let all that is within me cry, 'Worthy' . . . 'Jesus' . . . 'glory'

134 Let me have My way

G. Kendrick

Thoughtfully

1. Let Me have My way a - mong you, Do not strive, do not strive. strive. For Mine is the pow-er and the glo - ry For ev-er and ev-er the same.

Let Me have My way a - mong you, do not strive, Do not strive.

2 We'll let You have Your way among us,
We'll not strive, we'll not strive *Repeat*
For Yours is the power and the glory
For ever and ever the same.
We'll let You have Your way among us,
We'll not strive, we'll not strive.

3 Let My peace rule within your hearts,
Do not strive, do not strive *Repeat*
For Mine is the power and the glory
For ever and ever the same.
Let My peace rule within your hearts,
Do not strive, do not strive.

4 We'll let Your peace rule within our hearts,
We'll not strive, we'll not strive *Repeat*
For Yours. . . *etc.*

135 Let all the world

LUCKINGTON 10.4.66.66.10.4

Basil Harwood (1859-1949)

1 Let all the world in every corner sing
    "My God and King!"
  The heavens are not too high;
    His praise may thither fly:
  The earth is not too low;
    His praises there may grow.
  Let all the world in every corner sing
    "My God and King!"

2 Let all the world in every corner sing
    "My God and King!"
  The Church with psalms must shout,
    No door can keep them out:
  But, above all, the heart
    Must bear the longest part.
  Let all the world in every corner sing
    "My God and King!"

George Herbert 1593-1633

136 Let the beauty of Jesus

Albert Orsborn

Arr. Rev. Tom Jones

Let the beau-ty of Je-sus be seen in me,
All His won-drous com-pas-sion and pu-ri-ty,
Oh, Thou Spi-rit Di-vine, All my na-ture re-fine,
Till the beau-ty of Je-sus be seen in me.

137   Let there be love

Capo 1 (E)

Triumphantly

D. Bilbrough

Let there be love shared a-mong us, let there be love in our eyes, May now Your love sweep this na-tion, Cause us O Lord to a-rise, Give us a fresh un-der-stand-ing of bro-ther-ly love that is real, Let there be love shared a-mong us, Let there be love.

138 Let's just praise the Lord!

Gloria Gaither
William J. Gaither

William J. Gaither

Capo 1

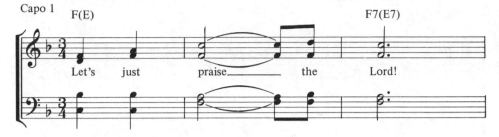

Let's just praise_____ the Lord!

Praise_____ the Lord! Let's just lift our hearts* to

heav - en and praise the Lord; Let's just

praise_____ the Lord! Praise_____ the Lord! Let's just

lift our hearts* to heav - en and praise the Lord!_____

* Alternate lyrics, "voices", "hands".

139 Lift high the cross

CRUCIFER 10 10 and refrain

S.H. Nicholson (1875-1947)

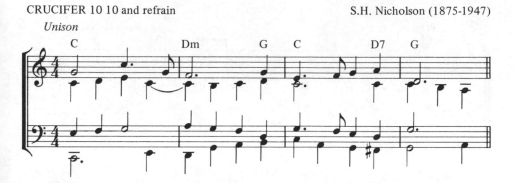

Lift high the cross, the love of Christ proclaim
Till all the world adores his sacred name!

1 Come, Christians, follow where the captain trod,
The king victorious, Christ the Son of God:
Lift high the cross. . . .

2 Each new-born soldier of the crucified
Bears on his brow the seal of him who died:
Lift high the cross. . . .

3 This is the sign that Satan's armies fear
And angels veil their faces to revere:
Lift high the cross. . . .

4 Saved by the cross on which their Lord was slain,
See Adam's children their lost home regain:
Lift high the cross. . . .

5 From north and south, from east and west they raise
In growing unison their songs of praise:
Lift high the cross. . . .

6 Let every race and every language tell
Of him who saves our souls from death and hell!
Lift high the cross. . . .

7 O Lord, once lifted on the tree of pain,
Draw all the world to seek you once again:
Lift high the cross. . . .

8 Set up your throne, that earth's despair may cease
Beneath the shadow of its healing peace:
Lift high the cross. . . .

G.W. Kitchen, 1827-1912
and M.R. Newbolt, 1874-1956

140 Like a river glorious

Frances R. Havergal 1836–79

J. Mountain

Capo 1

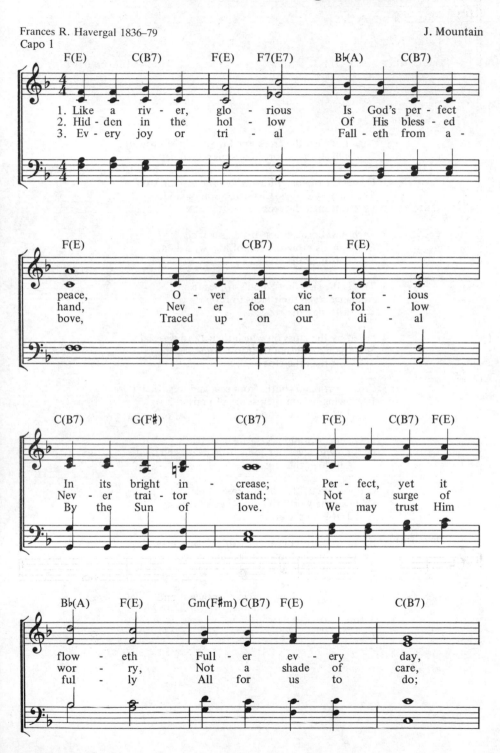

1. Like a riv - er, glo - rious Is God's per - fect peace, O - ver all vic - tor - ious In its bright in - crease; Per - fect, yet it flow - eth Full - er ev - ery day,

2. Hid - den in the hol - low Of His bless - ed hand, Nev - er foe can fol - low Nev - er trai - tor stand; Not a surge of wor - ry, Not a shade of care,

3. Ev - ery joy or tri - al Fall - eth from a - bove, Traced up - on our di - al By the Sun of love. We may trust Him ful - ly All for us to do;

208

F(E) C#dim(Cdim) Dm(C#m) G(F#)/B(A#) F(E)/C(B) C7(B7)

Per - fect, yet it grow - eth Deep - er all the
Not a blast of hur - ry Touch the Spi - rit
They who trust Him whol - ly Find Him whol - ly

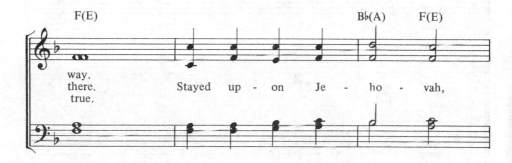

F(E) Bb(A) F(E)

way.
there. Stayed up - on Je - ho - vah,
true.

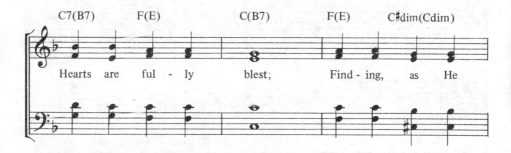

C7(B7) F(E) C(B7) F(E) C#dim(Cdim)

Hearts are ful - ly blest; Find - ing, as He

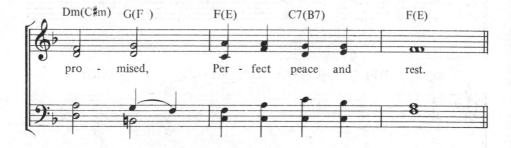

Dm(C#m) G(F) F(E) C7(B7) F(E)

pro - mised, Per - fect peace and rest.

141 Lo! He comes with clouds descending

HELMSLEY 8.7.8.7.4.7.

Select Hymns
with Tunes Annext (1765)

1 Lo! He comes with clouds descending,
   Once for favoured sinners slain;
Thousand thousand saints attending,
   Swell the triumph of His train:
     Hallelujah!
  God appears on earth to reign.

2 Every eye shall now behold Him
   Robed in dreadful majesty;
Those who set at nought and sold Him,
   Pierced and nailed Him to the tree,
     Deeply wailing,
  Shall the true Messiah see.

3 Now redemption, long expected,
   See in solemn pomp appear!
All His saints, by man rejected,
   Now shall meet Him in the air.
     Hallelujah!
  See the day of God appear.

4 Yea, Amen! Let all adore Thee,
   High on Thy eternal throne;
Saviour, take the power and glory,
   Claim the kingdom for Thine own;
     Hallelujah!
  Everlasting God, come down!

Charles Wesley, 1707-88

142 Lord, for the years

LORD OF THE YEARS 11 10 11 10

Michael Baughen (1930-)
arranged David Iliff (1939-)

1 Lord, for the years your love has kept and guided,
  Urged and inspired us, cheered us on our way,
  Sought us and saved us, pardoned and provided:
  Lord of the years, we bring our thanks today.

2 Lord, for that Word, the Word of life which fires us,
  Speaks to our hearts and sets our souls ablaze,
  Teaches and trains, rebukes us and inspires us:
  Lord of the Word, receive your people's praise.

3 Lord, for our land, in this our generation,
  Spirits oppressed by pleasure, wealth and care:
  For young and old, for commonwealth and nation,
  Lord of our land, be pleased to hear our prayer,

4 Lord, for our world, where men disown and doubt you,
  Loveless in strength, and comfortless in pain,
  Hungry and helpless, lost indeed without you:
  Lord of the world, we pray that Christ may reign.

5 Lord for ourselves; in living power remake us —
  Self on the cross and Christ upon the throne,
  Past put behind us, for the future take us:
  Lord of our lives, to live for Christ alone.

© *Timothy Dudley-Smith, 1926-*

143(i) Lord I was blind

SAXBY

T.R. Matthews (1826-1910)

143(ii)

GETTY
Capo 1

Alfred Scott Getty (1847-1918)

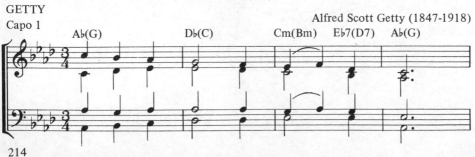

1 Lord, I was blind! I could not see
　In Thy marred visage any grace:
　But now the beauty of Thy face
In radiant vision dawns on me.

2 Lord, I was deaf! I could not hear
　The thrilling music of Thy voice;
　But now I hear Thee and rejoice,
And all Thine uttered words are dear.

3 Lord, I was dumb! I could not speak
　The grace and glory of Thy name;
　But now, as touched with living
　　flame,
My lips Thine eager praises wake.

4 Lord, I was dead! I could not stir
　My lifeless soul to come to Thee;
　But now, since Thou hast quickened
　　me,
I rise from sin's dark sepulchre.

5 For Thou hast made the blind to see,
　The deaf to hear, the dumb to speak,
　The dead to live; and lo, I break
The chains of my captivity!

William Tidd Matson 1833-99

144   Lord make me an instrument

T. Hatton
arr. R. Fudge

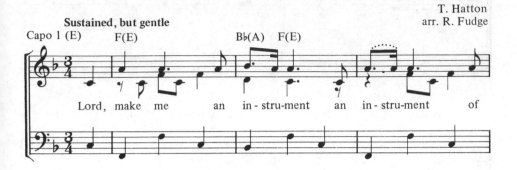

Lord, make me an in-stru-ment an in-stru-ment of

wor - ship I lift up my hands in Thy

na - me, Lord, make me an

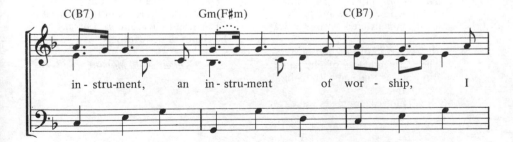

in - stru-ment, an in-stru-ment of wor - ship, I

lift up my hands in Thy Na - me.

2 I'll sing you a love song,
   A love song of worship;
   I lift up my hands in Thy name.
   I'll sing you a love song.
   A love song to Jesus;
   I lift up my hands in Thy name.

3 Lord, make us a symphony,
   A symphony of worship;
   We lift up our hands in Thy name,
   Lord, make us a symphony,
   A symphony of worship;
   We lift up our hands in Thy name.

145 Like a mighty river flowing

OLD YEAVERING 8 8 8 7   Noël Tredinnick (1949-)

© Noël Tredinnick

1 Like a mighty river flowing,
  Like a flower in beauty growing,
  Far beyond all human knowing
     Is the perfect peace of God.

2 Like the hills serene and even,
  Like the coursing clouds of heaven,
  Like the heart that's been forgiven
     Is the perfect peace of God.

3 Like the summer breezes playing,
  Like the tall trees softly swaying,
  Like the lips of silent praying
     Is the perfect peace of God.

4 Like the morning sun ascended,
  Like the scents of evening blended,
  Like a friendship never ended
     Is the perfect peace of God.

5 Like the azure ocean swelling,
  Like the jewel all-excelling,
  Far beyond our human telling
     Is the perfect peace of God.

   © *Michael Perry 1942-*

146   Lord may we see

JERUSALEM (D.C.M.)

C. Hubert H. Parry (1848 - 1918)
arr. Roland Fudge

Slow, but with animation

1 Lord may we see your hands and side
   Touch you and feel your presence near
   Lord could our eyes behold those clouds
   And watch you rising disappear.
   Help us to pray for your return
   To watch until you come to reign
   And be your witnesses through the world
   To speak and glorify your name.

2 Lord unto you we lift our eyes
   Help us to live as you desire
   Bring down upon us power to win
   Through tongues of Holy Spirit fire.
   Lord breathe upon us to receive
   The grace and love your Spirit gives
   And may we know you with us now
   Because in us your Spirit lives.

© Christopher Porteous, 1935-

147 Lord of the cross of shame

Michael Baughen (1930-)

1 Lord of the cross of shame,
   Set my cold heart aflame
   With love for you, my saviour and my master;
       Who on that lonely day
       Bore all my sins away,
   And saved me from the judgement and disaster.

2 Lord of the empty tomb,
   Born of a virgin's womb,
   Triumphant over death, its power defeated;
       How gladly now I sing
       Your praise, my risen king,
   And worship you, in heaven's splendour seated.

3 Lord of my life today,
   Teach me to live and pray
   As one who knows the joy of sins forgiven;
       So may I ever be,
       Now and eternally,
   One with my fellow-citizens in heaven.

© Michael Saward 1932-

148   Lord, speak to me

WHITBURN

H. Baker (1835-1910)

1 Lord, speak to me, that I may speak
       In living echoes of Thy tone;
    As Thou hast sought, so let me seek
       Thy erring children lost and lone.

2 O lead me, Lord, that I may lead
       The wandering and the wavering feet;
    O feed me, Lord, that I may feed
       Thy hungering ones with manna sweet.

3 O strengthen me, that, while I stand
       Firm on the rock, and strong in Thee,
    I may stretch out a loving hand
       To wrestlers with the troubled sea.

4 O teach me, Lord, that I may teach
       The precious things Thou dost impart;
    And wing my words, that they may reach
       The hidden depths of many a heart.

5 O give Thine own sweet rest to me,
       That I may speak with soothing power
    A word in season, as from Thee,
       To weary ones in needful hour.

6 O fill me with Thy fullness, Lord,
       Until my very heart o'erflow
    In kindling thought and glowing word,
       Thy love to tell, Thy praise to show.

7 O use me, Lord, use even me,
       Just as Thou wilt, and when, and where,
    Until Thy blessèd face I see,
       Thy rest, Thy joy, Thy glory share.

Frances Ridley Havergal 1836-79

149 Love divine

BLAENWERN 8 7 8 7 D   W.P. Rowlands (1860-1937)

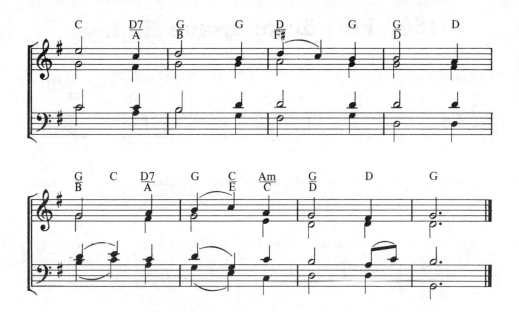

1 Love divine, all loves excelling,
    Joy of heaven, to earth come down,
Fix in us Thy humble dwelling,
    All Thy faithful mercies crown:
Jesus, Thou art all compassion,
    Pure, unbounded love Thou art;
Visit us with Thy salvation,
    Enter every trembling heart.

2 Breathe, O breathe Thy loving Spirit
    Into every troubled breast;
Let us all in Thee inherit,
    Let us find Thy promised rest;
Take away the love of sinning,
    Alpha and omega be;
End of faith, as its beginning,
    Set our hearts at liberty.

3 Come, almighty to deliver,
    Let us all Thy grace receive;
Suddenly return, and never,
    Never more Thy temples leave.
Thee we would be always blessing,
    Serve Thee as Thy hosts above,
Pray, and praise Thee without ceasing,
    Glory in Thy perfect love.

4 Finish, then, Thy new creation:
    Pure and spotless let us be;
Let us see Thy great salvation,
    Perfectly restored in Thee,
Changed from glory into glory,
    Till in heaven we take our place,
Till we cast our crowns before Thee,
    Lost in wonder, love, and praise.

Charles Wesley 1707-88

150 Low in the grave He lay

CHRIST AROSE 6.5.6.4. and refrain.

R. Lowry (1826-99)

Capo 1

228

1   Low in the grave He lay,
         Jesus, my Saviour;
       Waiting the coming day,
         Jesus, my Lord.

        Up from the grave He arose,
        With a mighty triumph o'er His foes;
     He arose a Victor from the dark domain,
     And He lives for ever with His saints to reign:
       He arose! He arose! Hallelujah! Christ arose!

2   Vainly they watch His bed,
         Jesus, my Saviour;
       Vainly they seal the dead,
         Jesus, my Lord.

3   Death cannot keep his prey,
         Jesus, my Saviour;
       He tore the bars away,
         Jesus, my Lord.

           Robert Lowry, 1826-99

151 Majesty

Jack W. Hayford

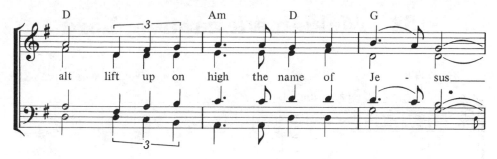

alt lift up on high the name of Je - sus

mag - ni - fy come glo - ri - fy Christ Je - sus the

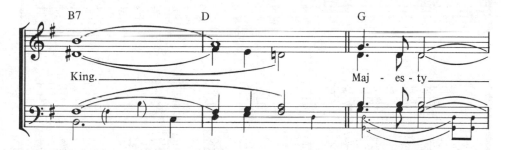

King. Maj - es - ty

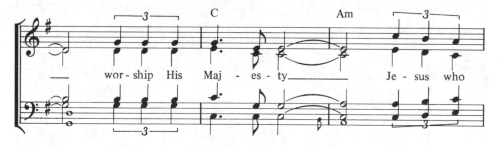

wor - ship His Maj - es - ty Je - sus who

died now glo - ri - fied King of all kings.

231

152 Make me a captive, Lord

LEOMINSTER

George William Martin (1828-81)

For alternative tune see No. 207

1   Make me a captive, Lord,
       And then I shall be free;
  Force me to render up my sword,
       And I shall conqueror be.
       I sink in life's alarms
       When by myself I stand;
  Imprison me within Thine arms,
       And strong shall be my hand.

2   My heart is weak and poor
       Until it master find;
  It has no spring of action sure —
       It varies with the wind.
       It cannot freely move,
       Till Thou hast wrought its chain;
  Enslave it with Thy matchless love,
       And deathless it shall reign.

3   My power is faint and low
       Till I have learned to serve;
  It wants the needed fire to glow,
       It wants the breeze to nerve;
       It cannot drive the world,
       Until itself be driven;
  Its flag can only be unfurled
       When Thou shalt breathe from heaven.

4   My will is not my own
       Till Thou hast made it Thine;
  If it would reach a monarch's throne
       It must its crown resign;
       It only stands unbent,
       Amid the clashing strife,
  When on Thy bosom it has leant
       And found in Thee its life.

George Matheson 1842-1906

153 Make me a channel of your peace

PRAYER OF ST. FRANCIS

Sebastian Temple
Arr. Betty Pulkingham

1. Make me a chan-nel of your peace.___ Where
2. Make me a chan-nel of your peace.___ Where
3. Make me a chan-nel of your peace.___ It

there is hat-red let me bring your love;___ where
there's des-pair in life let me bring hope;___ where
is in par-don-ing that we are par - doned,___ in

there is in-jur - y, your par-don, Lord;___ and___
there is dark-ness,___ on - ly light;___ and___
giv-ing to all men that we re - ceive;___ and in

where there's doubt, true faith in you.
where there's sad-ness, ev - er joy.
dy - ing that we're born to e-ter - nal life.

Oh,

mas-ter, grant that I may nev - er seek so

much to be con - soled as to con - sole; to be

un - der-stood as to un - der - stand; to be

loved, as to love with all my soul.

* Voices may sing in two-part harmony.

235

154 Man of sorrows!

GETHSEMANE 7 7 7.8.

P. Bliss (1838-76)

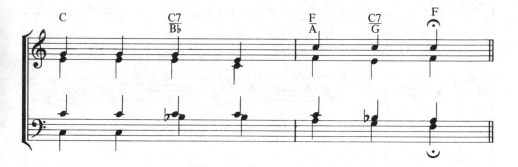

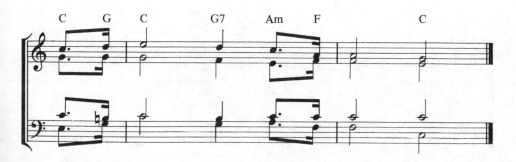

1 Man of Sorrows! What a name
   For the Son of God, who came
   Ruined sinners to reclaim!
       Hallelujah! what a Saviour!

2 Bearing shame and scoffing rude,
   In my place condemned He stood;
   Sealed my pardon with His blood:
       Hallelujah, what a Saviour!

3 Guilty, vile, and helpless we;
   Spotless Lamb of God was He:
   Full atonement — can it be?
       Hallelujah! what a Saviour!

4 Lifted up was He to die.
   It is finished! was His cry;
   Now in heaven exalted high;
       Hallelujah! what a Saviour!

5 When He comes, our glorious King,
   All His ransomed home to bring,
   Then anew this song we'll sing:
       Hallelujah! what a Saviour!

Philipp Bliss, 1838-76

155 Master speak!

MAGISTER 87.87.77

L. Mason (1792-1872)

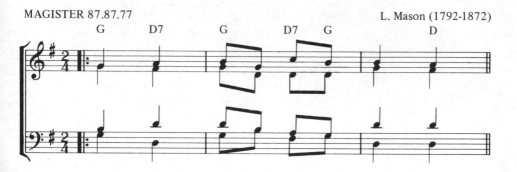

1 Master, speak! Thy servant heareth,
    Waiting for Thy gracious word,
  Longing for Thy voice that cheereth;
    Master, let it now be heard,
  I am listening, Lord, for Thee;
    What hast Thou to say to me?

2 Speak to me by name, O Master!
    Let me know it is to me;
  Speak, that I may follow faster,
    With a step more firm and free,
  Where the Shepherd leads the flock
    In the shadow of the rock.

3 Master, speak! though least and lowest,
    Let me not unheard depart;
  Master, speak! for O Thou knowest
    All the yearning of my heart;
  Knowest all its truest need;
    Speak, and make me blest indeed.

4 Master, speak! and make me ready,
    When Thy voice is truly heard,
  With obedience glad and steady
    Still to follow every word,
  I am listening, Lord, for Thee;
    Master, speak, O speak to me!

Frances Ridley Havergal 1836-79

156 May God's blessing

Words and Music by Cliff Barrows

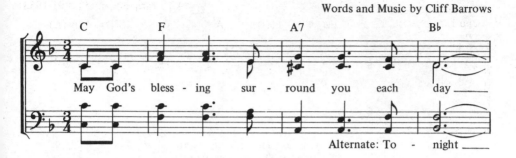

May God's bless - ing sur - round you each day

Alternate: To - night

As you trust Him and walk in His way

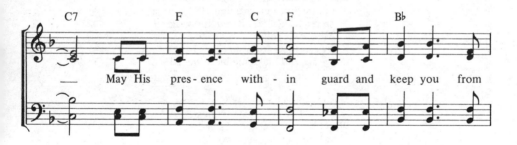

May His pres - ence with - in guard and keep you from

sin, Go in peace, go in joy, go in love.

157 May the mind of Christ my Saviour

ST. LEONARDS 87.85

A.C. Barham Gould (1891-1953)

1 May the mind of Christ my Saviour
   Live in me from day to day,
By His love and power controlling
   All I do or say.

2 May the word of God dwell richly
   In my heart from hour to hour,
So that all may see I triumph
   Only through His power.

3 May the peace of God my Father
   Rule my life in everything,
That I may be calm to comfort
   Sick and sorrowing.

4 May the love of Jesus fill me,
   As the waters fill the sea;
Him exalting, self abasing,
   This is victory.

5 May I run the race before me,
   Strong and brave to face the foe,
Looking only unto Jesus
   As I onward go.

   Kate B. Wilkinson 1859-1928

158 My faith looks up to Thee

OLIVET 664.6664
Capo 1

Lowell Mason (1792-1872)

1 My faith looks up to Thee,
Thou Lamb of Calvary,
  Saviour divine:
Now hear me while I pray;
Take all my guilt away;
O let me from this day
  Be wholly Thine.

2 May Thy rich grace impart
Strength to my fainting heart,
  My zeal inspire.
As Thou hast died for me,
O may my love to Thee
Pure, warm, and changeless be,
  A living fire.

3 While life's dark maze I tread,
And griefs around me spread,
  Be Thou my guide;
Bid darkness turn to day,
Wipe sorrow's tears away,
Nor let me ever stray
  From Thee aside.

4 When ends life's transient dream,
When death's cold sullen stream
  Shall o'er me roll,
Blest Saviour, then in love,
Fear and distrust remove;
O bear me safe above,
  A ransomed soul.

Ray Palmer, 1808-87

242

159 My soul doth magnify the Lord

Luke 1: 46-47, 49

Gently

Composer and author unknown
Arr. Betty Pulkingham

My soul doth mag-ni-fy_ the Lord, and my spi-rit hath re-joiced in God my
sa-viour for_ he that is might-y hath done great things, and ho-ly is his
name. My soul doth mag-ni-fy the Lord, my soul doth mag-ni-fy the Lord, and my
spi-rit hath re-joiced in God my sa-viour for_ he that is migh-ty hath done
great things, and ho-ly is his name. My soul doth name.

160 My song is love unknown

LOVE UNKNOWN 6.6.6.6.4.4.4.4.   J. Ireland

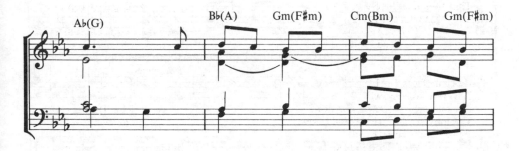

1 My song is love unknown;
My Saviour's love to me;
Love to the loveless shown,
That they may lovely be.
    O who am I,
        That for my sake,
        My Lord should take
    Frail flesh, and die?

2 He came from His blest Throne,
Salvation to bestow:
But men made strange, and none
The longed-for Christ would know.
    But O my friend!
        My Friend indeed,
        Who at my need
    His life did spend.

3 Sometimes they strew His way,
And His sweet praises sing;
Resounding all the day,
Hosannas to their King.
    Then: Crucify!
        Is all their breath,
        And for His death
    They thirst and cry.

4 Why, what hath my Lord done?
What makes this rage and spite?
He made the lame to run,
He gave the blind their sight.

Sweet injuries!
    Yet they at these
        Themselves displease,
    And 'gainst Him rise.

5 They rise and needs will have
My dear Lord made away;
A murderer they save;
The Prince of life they slay.
    Yet cheerful He
        To suffering goes,
        That He His foes
    From thence might free.

6 In life, no house, no home
My Lord on earth might have;
In death, no friendly tomb
But what a stranger gave.
    What may I say?
        Heav'n was His home;
        But mine the tomb
    Wherein He lay.

7 Here might I stay and sing,
No story so divine;
Never was love, dear King,
Never was grief like Thine.
    This is my Friend,
        In whose sweet praise
        I all my days
    Could gladly spend.

Samuel Crossman c. 1624-83

251

161 New every morning

MELCOMBE 8 8 8 8 (LM) S. Webbe (1740-1816)

1 New every morning is the love
　Our waking and uprising prove:
　Through sleep and darkness safely brought,
　Restored to life and power and thought.

2 New mercies, each returning day,
　Surround your people as they pray:
　New dangers past, new sins forgiven,
　New thoughts of God, new hopes of heaven.

3 If in our daily life our mind
　Be set to honour all we find,
　New treasures still, of countless price,
　God will provide for sacrifice.

4 The trivial round, the common task,
　Will give us all we ought to ask:
　Room to deny ourselves, a road
　To bring us daily nearer God.

5 Prepare us, Lord, in your dear love
　For perfect rest with you above,
　And help us, this and every day,
　To grow more like you as we pray.

J. Keble, 1792-1866

162(i) My hope is built

He H.F. Hemy (1818-1888)

H.F. Hemy (1818-1888)
Adapted by J.G. Walton (1821-1905)

ST. CATHERINE 8 8 8 8 8 8

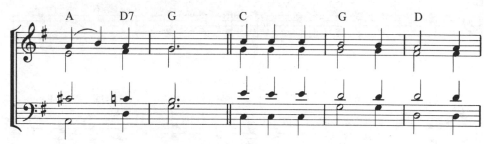

162(ii)

Edward Mote

William B. Bradbury

On Christ, the sol - id Rock, I stand; All oth - er ground is sink - ing sand, All oth - er ground is sink - ing sand.

1 My hope is built on nothing less
   Than Jesus' blood and righteousness;
   No merit of my own I claim,
   But wholly trust in Jesus' name.
         On Christ, the solid rock, I stand —
         All other ground is sinking sand.

2 When weary in this earthly race,
   I rest on his unchanging grace;
   In every wild and stormy gale
   My anchor holds and will not fail.
         On Christ, the solid rock. . .

3 His vow, his covenant and blood
   Are my defence against the flood;
   When earthly hopes are swept away
   He will uphold me on that day.
         On Christ, the solid rock. . .

4 When the last trumpet's voice shall sound,
   O may I then in him be found!
   Clothed in his righteousness alone,
   Faultless to stand before his throne.
         On Christ the solid rock. . .

E. Mote, 1797-1874
Words © in this version Jubilate Hymns

163   Now thank we all our God

NUN DANKET 6.7.6.7.6.6.6.6.
Capo 3

J. Crüger (1598-1662)

1 Now thank we all our God,
    With hearts, and hands, and voices;
Who wondrous things hath done,
    In whom His world rejoices;
Who, from our mothers' arms,
    Hath blessed us on our way
With countless gifts of love,
    And still is ours today.

2 O may this bounteous God
    Through all our life be near us,
With ever-joyful hearts
    And blessèd peace to cheer us,
And keep us in His grace,
    And guide us when perplexed,
And free us from all ills
    In this world and the next.

3 All praise and thanks to God
    The Father now be given,
The Son, and Him who reigns
    With Them in highest heaven:
The one, eternal God,
    Whom earth and heaven adore;
For thus it was, is now,
    And shall be evermore.

Martin Rinkart 1586-1649
tr. by Katherine Winkworth 1829-78

164 O Breath of life

SPIRITUS VITAE 9 8 9 8   Mary J. Hammond (1878-1964)

1 O Breath of life, come sweeping through us,
   Revive your church with life and power;
   O Breath of life, come, cleanse, renew us
   And fit your church to meet this hour.

2 O Breath of love, come breathe within us,
   Renewing thought and will and heart;
   Come, love of Christ, afresh to win us,
   Revive your church in every part!

3 O Wind of God, come bend us, break us
   Till humbly we confess our need;
   Then, in your tenderness remake us,
   Revive, restore — for this we plead.

Elizabeth A.P. Head, 1850-1936

165 O come let us adore Him

ADESTE FIDELES

J. Wade (c. 1711 - 86)
Arr. Roland Fudge

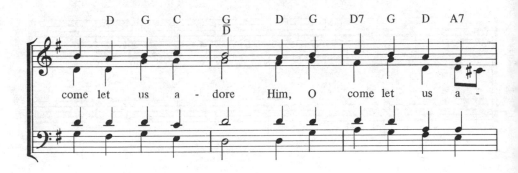

O come let us a - dore Him, O

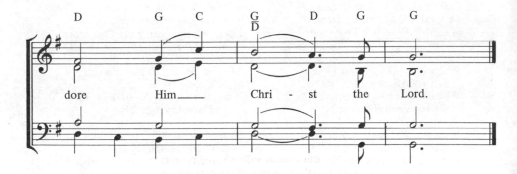

come let us a - dore Him, O come let us a -

dore Him____ Chri - st the Lord.

166(i)   O for a closer walk

CHESHIRE C.M.

Este's *Psalter*, 1592

1 O for a closer walk with God,
   A calm and heavenly frame,
 A light to shine upon the road
   That leads me to the Lamb.

2 Where is the blessedness I knew
   When first I saw the Lord?
 Where is that soul-refreshing view
   Of Jesus and His word?

3 What peaceful hours I once enjoyed!
   How sweet their memory still!
 But they have left an aching void
   The world can never fill.

4 Return, O holy dove! return,
   Sweet messenger of rest!
 I hate the sins that made Thee mourn,
   And drove Thee from my breast.

5 The dearest idol I have known,
   Whate'er that idol be,
 Help me to tear it from Thy throne,
   And worship only Thee.

6 So shall my walk be close with God,
   Calm and serene my frame;
 So purer light shall mark the road
   That leads me to the Lamb.

William Cowper, 1731-1800

254

166(ii)

MARTYRDOM 8 6 8 6 (CM)

H. Wilson (1760-1824)

167(i) O for a heart to praise my God

ABRIDGE C.M.

I. Smith (*c.* 1730-1800)

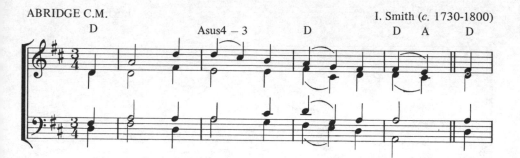

STOCKTON C.M.   **167(ii)**   T. Wright (1763-1829)

1 O for a heart to praise my God,
  A heart from sin set free,
A heart that always feels Thy blood
  So freely shed for me.

2 A heart resigned, submissive, meek,
  My great Redeemer's throne,
Where only Christ is heard to speak,
  Where Jesus reigns alone:

3 A humble, lowly, contrite heart,
  Believing, true, and clean;
Which neither life nor death can part
  From Him that dwells within:

4 A heart in every thought renewed,
  And full of love divine;
Perfect, and right, and pure, and good,
  A copy, Lord, of Thine.

5 Thy nature, gracious Lord, impart;
  Come quickly from above,
Write Thy new name upon my heart,
  Thy new, best name of love.

Charles Wesley, 1707-88

168 O for a thousand tongues

LYNGHAM 8 6 8 6 Extended

T. Jarman (1782-1862)

258

1 O for a thousand tongues to sing
        My great Redeemer's praise,
    The glories of my God and King,
        The triumphs of His grace!

2 Jesus! The name that charms our fears,
        That bids our sorrows cease;
    'Tis music in the sinner's ears,
        'Tis life, and health, and peace.

3 He breaks the power of cancelled sin,
        He sets the prisoner free;
    His blood can make the foulest clean;
        His blood availed for me.

4 He speaks, and, listening to His voice,
        New life the dead receive,
    The mournful, broken hearts rejoice,
        The humble poor believe.

5 Hear Him, ye deaf; His praise, ye dumb,
        Your loosened tongues employ:
    Ye blind, behold your Saviour come;
        And leap, ye lame, for joy.

6 My gracious Master and my God,
        Assist me to proclaim,
    To spread through all the earth abroad,
        The honours of Thy name.

Charles Wesley 1707-88 , altd.

169 O happy day!

P. Doddridge 1702–51
CAPO 1st Fret

Ron Jones

1. O hap-py day! — that fixed my choice — On Thee, my
2. 'Tis done, the great — tran-sac-tion's done! — I am my
3. Now rest, my long — di-vid-ed heart, — Fixed on this
4. High heav'n, that heard — the sol-emn vow, — That vow re-

Sav-iour and my God! — Well may this glow-ing heart re-
Lord's, and He is mine! — He drew me, and — I fol-lowed
bliss-ful cen-tre, rest; — Nor ev-er from — thy Lord de-
newed shall dai-ly hear; — Till in life's lat-est hour I

joice, — And tell its rap-tures all a-broad. —
on, — Charmed to con-fess the voice di-vine. —
part, — With Him of ev-'ry good pos-sessed. —
bow, — And bless in death a bond so dear. —

O hap-py day, — O hap-py day, — When Je-sus washed my sins a-

way; ___ He taught me how ___ to watch and pray, ___ And live re-

joic-ing ev-'ry day; ___ hal-le-lu-jah! O hap-py day, ___ O hap-py

day, ___ When Je-sus wash'd my sins a - way. ___

170 O Holy Spirit breathe on me

Norman Warren

1. O Ho-ly Spi - rit _ breathe on me, _ O Ho-ly Spi - rit _ breathe on me, _ and cleanse a-way my sin, _ fill me with love with-in:
_ O Ho-ly Spi - rit _ breathe on me.

2 O Holy Spirit fill my life,
O Holy Spirit fill my life,
Take all my pride from me,
Give me humility:
O Holy Spirit breathe on me!

3 O Holy Spirit make me new,
O Holy Spirit make me new,
Make Jesus real to me,
Give me his purity:
O Holy Spirit breathe on me!

4 O Holy Spirit wind of God,
O Holy Spirit wind of God,
Give me your power today,
To live for you always:
O Holy Spirit breathe on me!

171 O love that wilt not let me go

ST. MARGARET 88.886
Capo 1 (G)

A.L. Peace (1844-1912)

1 O Love that wilt not let me go,
   I rest my weary soul in Thee;
I give Thee back the life I owe,
That in Thine ocean depths its flow
   May richer, fuller be.

2 O Light that followest all my way,
   I yield my flickering torch to Thee;
My heart restores its borrowed ray,
That in Thy sunshine's blaze its day
   May brighter, fairer be.

3 O Joy that seekest me through pain,
   I cannot close my heart to Thee;
I trace the rainbow through the rain,
And feel the promise is not vain
   That morn shall tearless be.

4 O Cross that liftest up my head,
   I dare not ask to fly from Thee;
I lay in dust life's glory dead,
And from the ground there blossoms
   red
   Life that shall endless be.

George Matheson, 1842-1906

172 O Jesus, I have promised

DAY OF REST 76.76.D

Capo 3

J.W. Elliott (1833-1915)

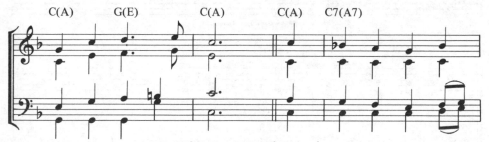

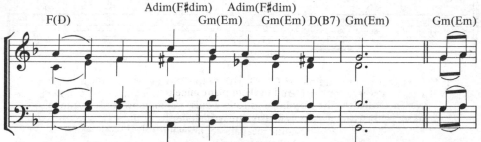

1 O Jesus, I have promised
   To serve Thee to the end;
Be Thou for ever near me,
   My master and my friend:
I shall not fear the battle
   If Thou art by my side,
Nor wander from the pathway
   If Thou wilt be my guide.

2 O let me feel Thee near me:
   The world is ever near;
I see the sights that dazzle,
   The tempting sounds I hear;
My foes are ever near me,
   Around me and within;
But, Jesus, draw Thou nearer,
   And shield my soul from sin.

3 O let me hear Thee speaking
   In accents clear and still,
Above the storms of passion,
   The murmurs of self-will;
O speak to reassure me,
   To hasten or control;
O speak, and make me listen,
   Thou guardian of my soul.

4 O Jesus, Thou hast promised,
   To all who follow Thee,
That where Thou art in glory
   There shall Thy servant be;
And, Jesus, I have promised
   To serve Thee to the end;
O give me grace to follow
   My master and my friend.

5 O let me see Thy footmarks,
   And in them plant mine own;
My hope to follow duly
   Is in Thy strength alone:
O guide me, call me, draw me,
   Uphold me to the end;
And then in heaven receive me,
   My Saviour and my friend!

J.E. Bode 1816-74

173 O Lord my God!

(How Great Thou art)

Russian hymn tune
Words and music
Stuart K. Hine

HOW GREAT THOU ART
Majestically

1. O Lord my God! when I in awesome wonder
   Consider all the works Thy hand hath made,
   I see the stars, I hear the mighty thunder,
   Thy pow'r throughout the universe display'd:

   Then sings my soul, my Saviour God, to Thee,
   How great Thou art! How great Thou art!
   Then sings my soul, my Saviour God, to Thee,
   How great Thou art! How great Thou art!

2. When through the woods and forest glades I wander
   And hear the birds sing sweetly in the trees;
   When I look down from lofty mountain grandeur,
   And hear the brook, and feel the gentle breeze;

3. And when I think that God His Son not sparing,
   Sent Him to die — I scarce can take it in.
   That on the cross my burden gladly bearing,
   He bled and died to take away my sin:

4. When Christ shall come with shout of acclamation
   And take me home — what joy shall fill my heart!
   Then shall I bow in humble adoration
   And there proclaim, my God, how great Thou art!

Russian hymn
tr. © *1953 Stuart K. Hine*
Ps 8; Rom 5.9-11;1 Thess 4:16-17

Note: previous printings of this music book
contained this song in the key of C.

174　O Thou who camest from above

WILTON L.M.

S. Stanley (1767-1822)

1 O Thou who camest from above
　　The pure, celestial fire to impart,
Kindle a flame of sacred love
　　On the mean altar of my heart.

2 There let it for Thy glory burn,
　　With inextinguishable blaze;
And, trembling, to its source return
　　In humble love and fervent praise.

3 Jesus, confirm my heart's desire
　　To work and speak and think for
　　　　Thee;
Still let me guard the holy fire,
　　And still stir up Thy gift in me;

4 Ready for all Thy perfect will,
　　My acts of faith and love repeat,
Till death Thine endless mercies seal,
　　And make the sacrifice complete.

Charles Wesley 1707-88

175 On a hill far away

THE OLD RUGGED CROSS

Capo 1(A)

Rev. George Bennard

1. On a hill far a-way stood an old rug-ged cross, The em-blem of suf-f'ring and shame; And I love that old cross where the dear-est and best For a world of lost sin-ners was slain. So I'll cher-ish the old rug-ged
2. Oh, the old rug-ged cross, so de-spised by the world, Has a won-drous at-trac-tion for me; For the dear Lamb of God left His glo-ry a-bove To bear it to dark Cal-va-ry. To
3. In the old rug-ged cross, stained with blood so di-vine, A won-drous beau-ty I see; For 'twas on that old cross Je-sus suf-fered and died To par-don and sanc-ti-fy me. To
4. To the old rug-ged cross I will ev-er be true, Its shame and re-proach glad-ly bear; Then He'll call me some day to my home far a-way, Where His glo-ry for-ev-er I'll share. Where

cross Till my tro-phies at last I lay down; I will cling to the old rug-ged cross And ex-change it some day for a crown.

old rug-ged cross, cross, the old rug-ged cross,

176 O what a gift!

Capo 2 (Am)

Joyfully, with a driving rhythm

Pat Uhl Howard
Arr. Betty Pulkingham

Refrain

O what a gift! What a won-der-ful gift!_ Who can tell the won-ders of the Lord? Let us op - en our eyes, our ears, and our hearts; it is Christ the Lord, it is he!

1. In the still - ness of the night ___ when the
2. On the night be - fore he died ___ it was
3. On the hill of Cal - va - ry ___ the
4. Ear - ly on that morn - ing when the
5. Some day with the saints ___ we will

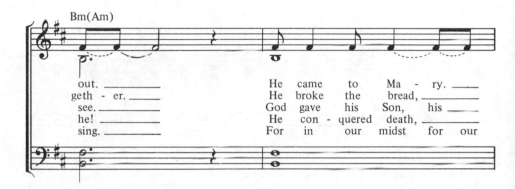

A(G)　　　　　　　　　　　G(F)　　　A(G)

world — was a - sleep, — the al - might- y ___ word ___ leapt ___
Pass - ov - er night, — and he gath - ered his friends _ to -
world — held its breath, for — there for the world ___ to ___
world — was — sleep - ing, _____ back to ___ life ____ came ___
come be-fore our Fa - ther — and then we will shout and dance and

Bm(Am)

out. _____　　　　　　　　He came to Ma - ry. ___
geth - er. _____　　　　　　He broke the bread, _____
see. _____　　　　　　　　　God gave his Son, his ___
he! _____　　　　　　　　　He con - quered death, _____
sing. _____　　　　　　　　For in our midst for our

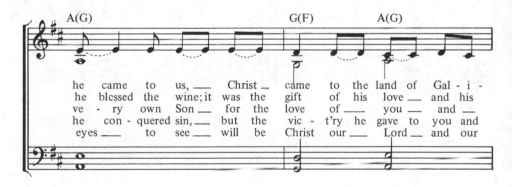

A(G)　　　　　　　　　　　G(F)　　　A(G)

he came to us, ___ Christ — came to the land of Gal - i -
he blessed the wine; it was the gift of his love ___ and his
ve - ry own Son ___ for the love of ___ you ___ and —
he con - quered sin, ___ but the vic - t'ry he gave to you and
eyes ___ to see ___ will be Christ our ___ Lord — and our

Bm(Am)　　　　　　　　　F♯m(Em)　　　Bm(Am) *Refrain*

lee.
life.
me.　　⎫
me!　　⎬　　　　　　　Christ our Lord and our King!
King.　⎭

271

177 O Word of God incarnate

BENTLEY 76.76.D
Capo 1 (C)

John Hullah (1812-84)

1 O Word of God incarnate,
  O wisdom from on high,
O truth unchanged, unchanging,
  O light of our dark sky,
We praise Thee for the radiance,
  That from the hallowed page,
A lantern to our footsteps,
  Shines on from age to age.

2 The Church from her dear Master
  Received the gift divine,
And still that light she lifteth
  O'er all the earth to shine:
It is the golden casket
  Where gems of truth are stored;
It is the heaven-drawn picture
  Of Christ, the living Word.

3 It floateth like a banner
  Before God's host unfurled
It shineth like a beacon
  Above the darkling world:
It is the chart and compass
  That o'er life's surging sea,
Mid mists and rocks and quicksands
  Still guide, O Christ, to Thee.

4 O make Thy Church, dear Saviour,
  A lamp of burnished gold,
To bear before the nations
  Thy true light as of old;
O teach Thy wandering pilgrims
  By this their path to trace,
Till, clouds and darkness ended,
  They see Thee face to face!

W.W. How 1823-97

178   O worship the King

HANOVER 55.55.65.65

W. Croft (1678-1727)

1 O worship the King,
   All-glorious above;
O gratefully sing
   His power and His love;
Our shield and defender,
   The ancient of days,
Pavilioned in splendour,
   And girded with praise.

2 O tell of His might,
   O sing of His grace,
Whose robe is the light,
   Whose canopy, space;
His chariots of wrath
   The deep thunder-clouds form,
And dark is His path
   On the wings of the storm.

3 The earth, with its store
   Of wonders untold,
Almighty, Thy power
   Hath founded of old:
Hath stablished it fast
   By a changeless decree,
And round it hath cast
   Like a mantle, the sea.

4 Thy bountiful care
   What tongue can recite?
It breathes in the air,
   It shines in the light,
It streams from the hills,
   It descends to the plain,
And sweetly distils
   In the dew and the rain.

5 Frail children of dust,
   And feeble as frail,
In Thee do we trust,
   Nor find Thee to fail:
Thy mercies, how tender,
   How firm to the end,
Our maker, defender,
   Redeemer, and friend!

6 O Lord of all might,
   How boundless Thy love!
While angels delight
   To hymn Thee above,
The humbler creation,
   Though feeble their lays,
With true adoration
   Shall sing to Thy praise.

Robert Grant 1779-1838

179 O worship the Lord

SANCTISSIMUS 12.10.12.10.

W.H. Cook (1889)

* This chord is for the first and last verses only.

1 O worship the Lord in the beauty of holiness!
     Bow down before Him, His glory proclaim;
  With gold of obedience and incense of lowliness,
     Kneel and adore Him, the Lord is His name.

2 Low at His feet lay thy burden of carefulness,
     High in His heart He will bear it for thee,
  Comfort thy sorrows, and answer thy prayerfulness,
     Guiding thy steps as may best for thee be.

3 Fear not to enter His courts in the slenderness
     Of the poor wealth thou wouldst reckon as thine:
  Truth in its beauty and love in its tenderness:
     These are the offerings to lay on His shrine.

4 These, though we bring them in trembling and fearfulness,
     He will accept for the name that is dear;
  Mornings of joy give for evenings of tearfulness,
     Trust for our trembling, and hope for our fear.

5 O worship the Lord in the beauty of holiness!
     Bow down before Him, His glory proclaim;
  With gold of obedience and incense of lowliness,
     Kneel and adore Him, the Lord is His name.

                    John Samuel Bewley Monsell 1811-75

180 One day when heaven

J. Wilbur Chapman 1859–1918

Chas. H. Marsh

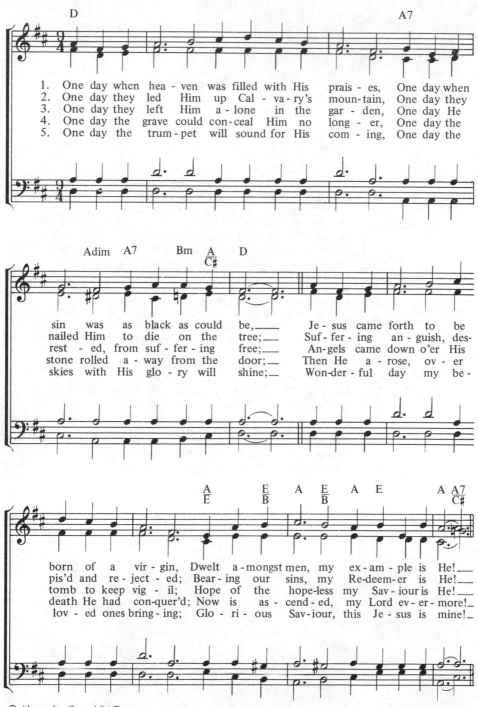

1. One day when heaven was filled with His prais-es, One day when
2. One day they led Him up Cal-va-ry's moun-tain, One day they
3. One day they left Him a-lone in the gar-den, One day He
4. One day the grave could con-ceal Him no long-er, One day the
5. One day the trum-pet will sound for His com-ing, One day the

sin was as black as could be,___ Je-sus came forth to be
nailed Him to die on the tree;___ Suf-fer-ing an-guish, des-
rest-ed, from suf-fer-ing free;___ An-gels came down o'er His
stone rolled a-way from the door;___ Then He a-rose, ov-er
skies with His glo-ry will shine;___ Won-der-ful day my be-

born of a vir-gin, Dwelt a-mongst men, my ex-am-ple is He!___
pis'd and re-ject-ed; Bear-ing our sins, my Re-deem-er is He!___
tomb to keep vig-il; Hope of the hope-less my Sav-iour is He!___
death He had con-quer'd; Now is as-cend-ed, my Lord ev-er-more!___
lov-ed ones bring-ing; Glo-ri-ous Sav-iour, this Je-sus is mine!___

181 Open our eyes, Lord

Robert Cure
Arr. David Peacock

O - pen our eyes, Lord, we

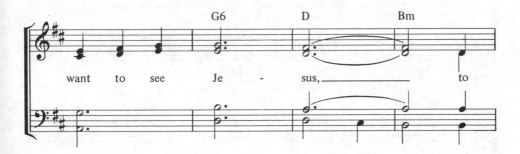

want to see Je - sus, to

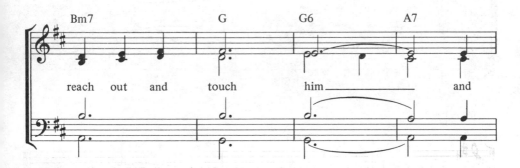

reach out and touch him and

say that we love him;

o - pen our ears Lord, _____ and

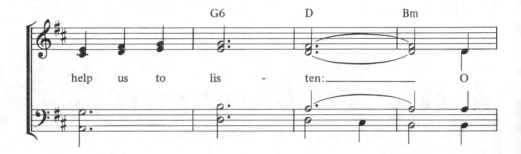

help us to lis - ten: _____ O

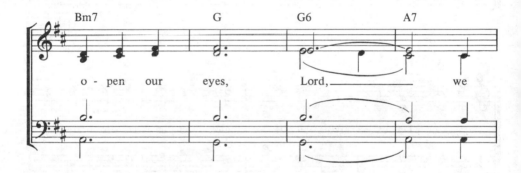

o - pen our eyes, Lord, _____ we

want to see Je - sus! _____

182 O give thanks to the Lord

O GIVE THANKS TO THE LORD

Joanne Pond
Arr. Roland Fudge

Lively
A7 D G D G
O give thanks to the Lord, all you his
D A7 D G D A E7
peo-ple O give thanks to the Lord for He is good.
A A7 D G D G
Let us praise, let us thank, let us cel - e - brate_and
D A7 D G D A7 D G D
dance; O give thanks to the Lord for He is good.

183   Peace is flowing like a river

Anon.
Arr. Betty Pulkingham

Peace is flow-ing like a riv - er,
Flow - ing out through you and me, ___ Spread-ing out in to the
des - ert, Set - ting all the cap-tives free.

Other verses may be added:

Love is flowing . . . Joy, Faith, Hope, *etc.*

184(i) Peace, perfect peace

George Thomas Calbeck (1852-1918)
and Charles Vincent (1852-1934)

PAX TECUM 10 10
Capo 1

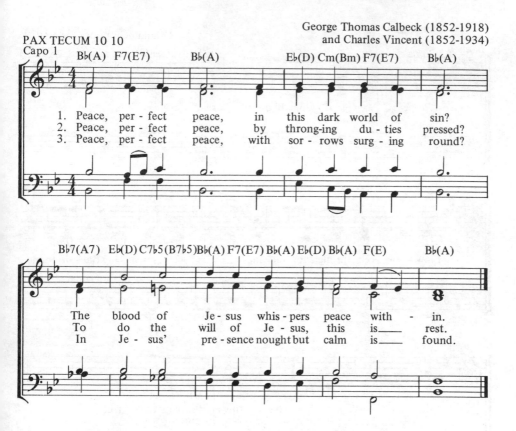

1. Peace, per-fect peace, in this dark world of sin?
2. Peace, per-fect peace, by throng-ing du-ties pressed?
3. Peace, per-fect peace, with sor-rows surg-ing round?

The blood of Je-sus whis-pers peace with-in.
To do the will of Je-sus, this is rest.
In Je-sus' pre-sence nought but calm is found.

4 Peace, perfect peace, with loved ones far away?
   In Jesus' keeping we are safe, and they.

5 Peace, perfect peace, our future all unknown?
   Jesus we know, and He is on the throne.

6 Peace, perfect peace, death shadowing us and ours?
   Jesus has vanquished death and all its powers.

7 It is enough: earth's struggles soon shall cease,
   And Jesus call us to heaven's perfect peace.

Edward Henry Bickersteth, 1825-1906

284

184(ii)

Orlando Gibbons (1583-1625)

1 Peace, perfect peace, in this dark world of sin?
The blood of Jesus whispers peace within.

2 Peace, perfect peace, by thronging duties pressed?
To do the will of Jesus, this is rest.

3 Peace, perfect peace, with sorrows surging round?
In Jesus' presence nought but calm is found.

4 Peace, perfect peace, with loved ones far away?
In Jesus' keeping we are safe, and they.

5 Peace, perfect peace, our future all unknown?
Jesus we know, and He is on the throne.

6 Peace, perfect peace, death shadowing us and ours?
Jesus has vanquished death and all its powers.

7 It is enough: earth's struggles soon shall cease,
And Jesus call us to heaven's perfect peace.

Edward Henry Bickersteth, 1825-1906

285

185 Praise God

DOXOLOGY
Thomas Ken

Jimmy Owens

With movement

Praise God from whom all bless - ings flow; Praise him all crea - tures here be - low. Praise him a - bove ye hea - ven-ly hosts; Praise Fa - ther, Son, and Ho - ly Ghost.

Optional 4-part setting

Praise God from whom all bless - ings flow; Praise

him all crea - tures here be - low. Praise

him a bove ye hea - ven - ly host; Praise
Praise him

Fa - ther, Son, and Ho - ly Ghost. Praise Ghost.

† One very attractive way to sing this song in parts:

First time: Sopranos begin
                      Add altos at mid-point*
Second time: Tenors join
                      Basses too (at mid-point)*
Third time: All sing

186 Praise Him! Praise Him!

12.10.12.10.11.10.12.10

C.G. Allen (1838-78)

288

1 Praise Him! praise Him! Jesus, our blessèd Redeemer!
    Sing, O earth — His wonderful love proclaim!
Hail Him! hail Him! highest archangels in glory;
    Strength and honour give to His holy name!
Like a shepherd, Jesus will guard His children,
    In His arms He carries them all day long.

     Praise Him! praise Him! tell of His excellent greatness;
     Praise Him! praise Him ever in joyful song!

2 Praise Him! praise Him! Jesus, our blessèd Redeemer!
    For our sins He suffered, and bled, and died;
He — our rock, our hope of eternal salvation,
    Hail Him! hail Him! Jesus, the Crucified!
Sound His praises — Jesus who bore our sorrows,
    Love unbounded, wonderful, deep, and strong.

3 Praise Him! praise Him! Jesus, our blessèd Redeemer!
    Heavenly portals, loud with hosannas ring!
Jesus, Saviour, reigneth for ever and ever:
    Crown Him! crown Him! prophet, and priest, and king!
Christ is coming, over the world victorious,
    Power and glory unto the Lord belong.

Frances van Alstyne 1820-1915

187 Praise, my soul

87.87.87.

J. Goss (1800-80)

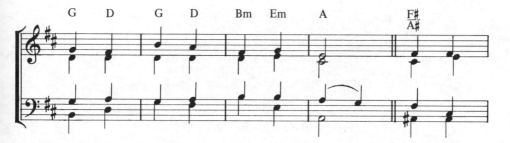

1 Praise, my soul, the King of heaven;
  To His feet thy tribute bring;
  Ransomed, healed, restored, forgiven,
  Who like thee His praise should sing?
  Praise Him, praise Him, praise Him, praise Him,
  Praise the everlasting King.

2 Praise Him for His grace and favour
  To our fathers in distress;
  Praise Him, still the same for ever,
  Slow to chide, and swift to bless:
  Praise Him! Praise Him! Praise Him! Praise Him!
  Glorious in His faithfulness.

3 Father-like He tends and spares us;
  Well our feeble frame He knows;
  In His hands He gently bears us,
  Rescues us from all our foes;
  Praise Him! Praise Him! Praise Him! Praise Him!
  Widely as His mercy flows.

4 Angels, help us to adore Him!
  Ye behold Him face to face;
  Sun and moon, bow down before Him;
  Dwellers all in time and space.
  Praise Him! Praise Him! Praise Him! Praise Him!
  Praise with us the God of grace.

H.F. Lyte 1793-1847

188 Praise the Lord!

Psalm 150: 1 – 3

Lee Abbey Music Workshop

From Sing Good News No. 1. Published by Bible Society.

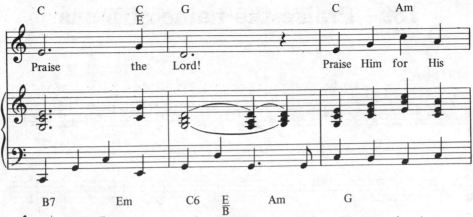

Praise the Lord! Praise Him for His

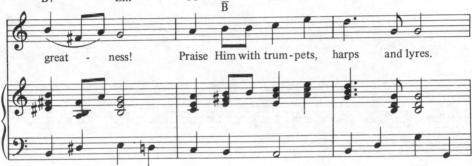

great - ness! Praise Him with trum-pets, harps and lyres.

All liv - ing crea - tures, praise! O praise, O

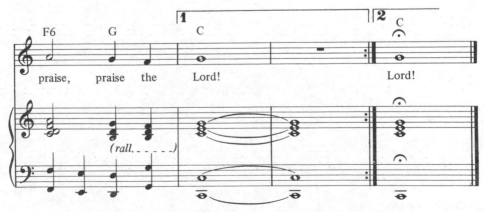

praise, praise the Lord! Lord!

189 Praise the name of Jesus

Words and Music by Roy Hicks

Praise the name of Je - sus Praise the name of Je - sus

He's my rock he's my fort - ress He's my de - liv - er - er in

Him will I trust Praise the name of Je - sus.

190 Prayer is the soul's sincere desire

NOX PRAECESSIT C.M.

J. Baptiste Calkin (1827-1905)

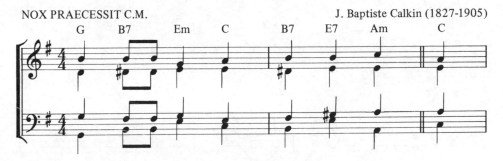

1 Prayer is the soul's sincere desire,
    Uttered or unexpressed,
The motion of a hidden fire
    That trembles in the breast.

2 Prayer is the burden of a sigh,
    The falling of a tear,
The upward glancing of an eye
    When none but God is near.

3 Prayer is the simplest form of speech
    That infant lips can try;
Prayer the sublimest strains that reach
    The Majesty on high.

4 Prayer is the contrite sinner's voice,
    Returning from his ways,
While angels in their songs rejoice,
    And cry, "Behold, he prays!"

5 Prayer is the Christian's vital breath,
    The Christian's native air,
His watchword at the gates of death;
    He enters heaven with prayer.

6 Nor prayer is made on earth alone;
    The Holy Spirit pleads;
And Jesus, on the eternal throne,
    For sinners intercedes.

7 O Thou by whom we come to God,
    The life, the truth, the way,
The path of prayer Thyself hast trod:
    Lord, teach us how to pray!

James Montgomery 1771-1854

191 Praise to the Holiest

GERONTIUS C.M.

J.B. Dykes (1823 - 76)

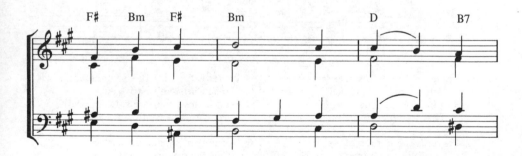

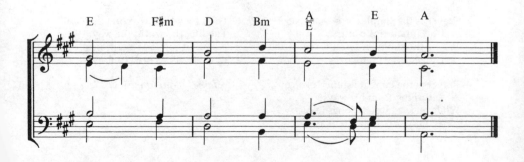

1 Praise to the Holiest in the height,
    And in the depth be praise:
In all His words most wonderful;
    Most sure in all His ways.

2 O loving wisdom of our God!
    When all was sin and shame,
A second Adam to the fight
    And to the rescue came.

3 O wisest love! that flesh and blood
    Which did in Adam fail,
Should strive afresh against the foe,
    Should strive and should prevail.

4 And that a higher gift than grace
    Should flesh and blood refine,
God's presence, and His very self
    And essence all-divine.

5 O generous love! that He, who smote
    In man for man the foe,
The double agony in man
    For man should undergo.

6 And in the garden secretly,
    And on the Cross on high,
Should teach His brethren, and inspire
    To suffer and to die.

7 Praise to the Holiest in the height,
    And in the depth be praise:
In all His words most wonderful;
    Most sure in all His ways.

John Henry Newman 1801-90

192 Praise to the Lord

Later form of melody in
Stralsund Gesangbuch, 1665
(as given in *The Chorale Book for England*, 1863)

LOBE DEN HERREN 14.14.478

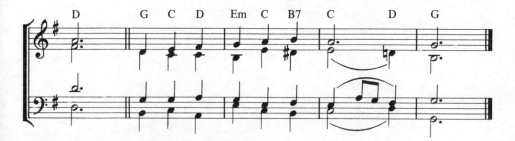

1 Praise to the Lord, the Almighty, the King of creation;
O my soul, praise Him, for He is thy health and salvation:
    All ye who hear,
    Brothers and sisters, draw near,
Praise Him in glad adoration.

2 Praise to the Lord, who o'er all things so wondrously reigneth,
Shelters thee under His wings, yea, so gently sustaineth:
    Hast thou not seen?
    All that is needful hath been
Granted in what He ordaineth.

3 Praise to the Lord, who doth prosper thy work, and defend thee!
Surely His goodness and mercy here daily attend thee:
    Ponder anew
    What the Almighty can do,
Who with His love doth befriend thee.

4 Praise to the Lord! O let all that is in me adore Him!
All that hath life and breath come now with praises before Him!
    Let the amen
    Sound from His people again:
Gladly for aye we adore Him.

Joachim Neander 1650-80
tr. Catherine Winkworth 1827-78 , and others

193   Reach out and touch the Lord

Capo 1 (E)

Bill Harmon

194 Rejoice in the Lord always

Text from Phil. 4:4
Music Traditional —
A round in 4 parts

Evelyn Tarner

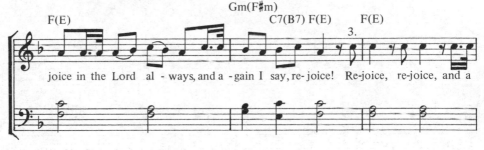

195 Rejoice, the Lord is King!

Handel (1685-1759)
(Composed for this hymn)

GOPSAL 6.6.6.6.8.8.

1 Rejoice, the Lord is King!
    Your Lord and King adore;
  Mortals, give thanks, and sing,
    And triumph evermore:

  Lift up your heart, lift up your voice;
  Rejoice; again I say, Rejoice.

2 Jesus the Saviour reigns,
    The God of truth and love;
  When He had purged our stains,
    He took His seat above:

3 His kingdom cannot fail,
    He rules o'er earth and heaven;
  The keys of death and hell
    Are to our Jesus given:

4 He sits at God's right hand,
    Till all His foes submit,
  And bow to His command,
    And fall beneath His feet:

5 Rejoice in glorious hope;
    Jesus the Judge shall come,
  And take His servants up
    To their eternal home:

  We soon shall hear the archangel's voice;
  The trump of God shall sound, Rejoice!

  Charles Wesley, 1707-88

196　Restore O Lord

Moderately fast

Graham Kendrick
Chris Rolinson

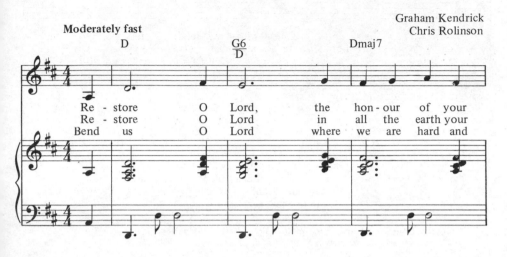

Re - store O Lord, the hon - our of your
Re - store O Lord in all the earth your
Bend us O Lord where we are hard and

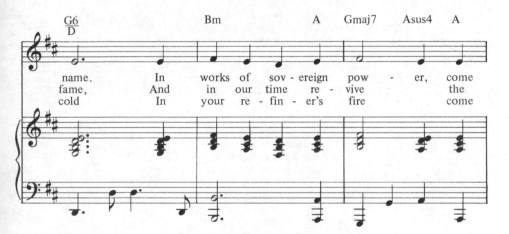

name. In works of sov - ereign pow - er, come
fame, And in our time re - vive the
cold In your re - fin - er's fire come

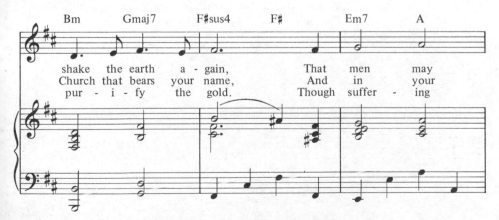

shake the earth a - gain, That men may
Church that bears your name, And in your
pur - i - fy the gold. Though suffer - ing

see, and come with rev-erent fear to the
anger, Lord re-mem-ber mer-cy Oh-
comes and ev-il crou-ches near Still our

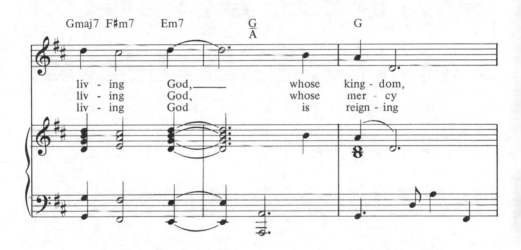

liv-ing God,_____ whose king-dom,
liv-ing God, whose mer-cy
liv-ing God is reign-ing

shall out-last the years. _____
shall out-last the years.
He is reign-ing here.

197(i)   Rock of ages

PETRA 7 7 7 7 7 7

R. Redhead (1820-1901)

1 Rock of Ages, cleft for me,
 Let me hide myself in Thee;
 Let the water and the blood,
 From Thy riven side which flowed,
 Be of sin the double cure,
 Cleanse me from its guilt and power.

2 Not the labour of my hands
 Can fulfil Thy law's demands;
 Could my zeal no respite know,
 Could my tears for ever flow,
 All for sin could not atone;
 Thou must save, and Thou alone.

3 Nothing in my hand I bring,
 Simply to Thy cross I cling;
 Naked, come to Thee for dress,
 Helpless, look to Thee for grace;
 Foul, I to the fountain fly,
 Wash me, Saviour, or I die.

4 While I draw this fleeting breath,
 When mine eyes shall close in death,
 When I soar through tracts unknown,
 See Thee on Thy judgment throne;
 Rock of ages, cleft for me,
 Let me hide myself in Thee.

A.M. Toplady, 1740-78

306

197(ii)

TOPLADY 7 7 7 7 7 7   A. Toplady (1740-1778)

Capo 1 (A)

198 Revive thy work, O Lord

SWABIA S.M.

Arr. by W.H. Havergal (1793-1870)
from a melody in J.M. Spiess' *Gesangbuch*, 1745

1 Revive Thy work, O Lord,
Thy mighty arm make bare;
Speak with the voice that wakes the
dead
And make Thy people hear.

2 Revive Thy work, O Lord,
Disturb this sleep of death;
Quicken the smouldering embers now
By Thine almighty breath.

3 Revive Thy work, O Lord,
Create soul-thirst for Thee;
And hungering for the bread of life
O may our spirits be!

4 Revive Thy work, O Lord,
Exalt Thy precious name;
And, by the Holy Ghost, our love
For Thee and Thine inflame.

5 Revive Thy work, O Lord,
Give pentecostal showers;
The glory shall be all Thine own,
The blessing, Lord, be ours.

Albert Midlane 1825-1909

199 Silver and gold

Anon.

Arr. Betty Pulkingham

Rollicking

Verse: Pe-ter and John went to pray,_they met a lame man on the way. He_
Refrain: 'Sil-ver and gold have I none,_but such as I have give I thee, in the

asked for alms_ and held out his palms,and this is what Pe-ter did
name of Je-sus Christ ____ of Naz-a-reth, rise up and

say: _____ walk!'_ He went walk-ing and leap-ing and

prais-ing God, walk-ing and leap-ing and prais-ing God. 'In the

name of Je-sus Christ _ of Naz-a-reth, rise up and walk.'___

309

200　Search me, O God

J. Edwin Orr
Capo 4

Arranged from an old
Maori melody

1 Search me, O God, and know my heart today;
  Try me, O Lord, and know my thoughts I pray:
  See if there be some wicked way in me,
  Cleanse me from ev'ry sin and set me free.

2 I praise Thee, Lord, for cleansing me from sin;
  Fulfil Thy Word, and make me pure within;
  Fill me with fire, where once I burned with shame
  Grant my desire to magnify Thy name.

3 Lord, take my life, and make it wholly Thine;
  Fill my poor heart with Thy great love divine;
  Take all my will, my passion, self and pride;
  I now surrender — Lord, in me abide.

4 O Holy Ghost, revival comes from Thee;
  Send a revival — start the work in me:
  Thy Word declares Thou wilt supply our need;
  For blessing now, O Lord, I humbly plead.

J. Edwin Orr

201 Seek ye first

Karen Lafferty
arr. Roland Fudge

Rich and broad

Seek ye first the King-dom of God,

and his right - eous - ness,

and all these things shall be add - ed un - to you.

Al - le - lu, al - le - lu ——— ia.

Man shall not live by bread alone,
But by every word,
That proceeds from the mouth of God.
Alleluia, Alleluia.

Ask and it shall be given unto you,
Seek and ye shall find,
Knock and the door shall be opened up to you.
Alleluia, Alleluia.

202 Seek ye the Lord

Joan Parsons
arr. Roland Fudge

1. Seek ye the Lord all ye peo - ple,_____ Turn to Him__ while He is near._____ Let__ the wick - ed for - sake his own way and call on Him while He may hear._____ Come with-out mo - ney and price. And there is peace

2. Ho ev - 'ry - one who is thir - sty,_____ Come to the__ wa - ters of life,_____ Come__ and drink of the milk and the wine,__ love

like a ri - ver_____ and glo - ry di -
ev - er flow - ing_____ and joy ev - er

vine, If you'll come to the wa - ter,
full, And there's life ev - er - last - ing

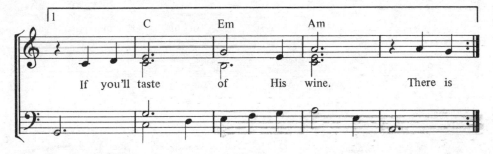

If you'll taste of His wine. There is

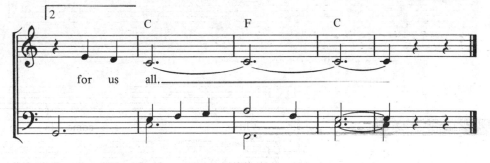

for us all,_____

203 Sing a new song

ONSLOW SQUARE 7 7 11 8

David G. Wilson (1940-   )

1. Sing a new song to the Lord, he to whom won-ders be-

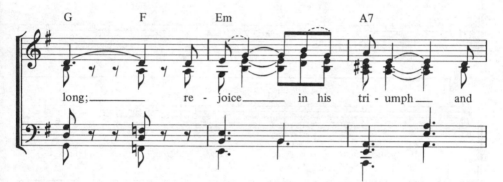

long;_____ re - joice_____ in his tri - umph_____ and

tell_____ of his power_____ O sing_____ to the

Lord_____ a new song!

2 Now to the ends of the earth
   See his salvation is shown;
   And still he remembers his mercy and truth
   Unchanging in love to his own.

3 Sing a new song and rejoice,
   Publish his praises abroad;
   Let voices in chorus, with trumpet and horn,
   Resound for the joy of the Lord!

4 Join with the hills and the sea
   Thunders of praise to prolong;
   In judgement and justice he comes to the earth —
   O sing to the Lord a new song!

204 Sing alleluia

Linda Strassen
Arr. Norman L. Warren

New Song Ministries, P.O. Box 11662 Costa Mesa, CA 92626 USA.

1 Sing alleluia to the Lord,
  Sing alleluia to the Lord,
  Sing alleluia, sing alleluia,
  Sing alleluia to the Lord!

2 Jesus is risen from the dead,
  Jesus is risen from the dead,
  Jesus is risen, Jesus is risen,
  Jesus is risen from the dead!

3 Jesus is Lord of heaven and earth,
  Jesus is Lord of heaven and earth,
  Jesus is Lord, Jesus is Lord,
  Jesus is Lord of heaven and earth,

4 Jesus is coming for his own,
  Jesus is coming for his own,
  Jesus is coming, Jesus is coming,
  Jesus is coming for his own.

Verse 1 © 1974 Linda Stassen
Verse 2–4 anonymous

205 Open Thou mine eyes

Psalm 119 v. 18.

C.C. Kerr

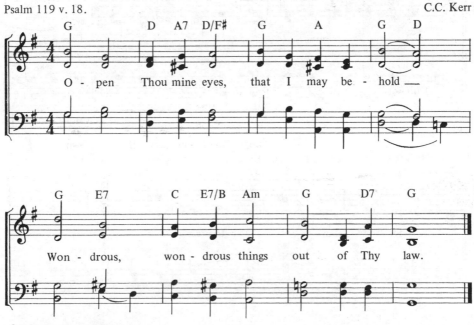

O - pen   Thou mine eyes,   that   I   may be - hold —

Won - drous,   won - drous things   out   of   Thy   law.

206 Sing we the king

C.H. Gabriel (1856-1932)

CHORUS
Come let us

1 Sing we the King who is coming to reign,
Glory to Jesus, the Lamb that was slain.
Life and salvation His empire shall bring.
Joy to the nations when Jesus is King.
Come let us sing: Praise to our King,
Jesus our King, Jesus our King:
This is our song, who to Jesus belong:
Glory to Jesus, to Jesus our King.

2 All men shall dwell in His marvellous light,
Races long severed His love shall unite,
Justice and truth from His sceptre shall spring,
Wrong shall be ended when Jesus is King.

3 All shall be well in His kingdom of peace,
Freedom shall flourish and wisdom increase,
Foe shall be friend when His triumph we sing,
Sword shall be sickle when Jesus is King.

4 Souls shall be saved from the burden of sin,
Doubt shall not darken His witness within,
Hell hath no terrors, and death hath no sting;
Love is victorious when Jesus is King.

5 Kingdom of Christ, for Thy coming we pray,
Hasten, O Father, the dawn of the day
When this new song Thy creation shall sing,
Satan is vanquished and Jesus is King.

C. Silvester Horne, 1865-1914

207 Soldiers of Christ, arise

FROM STRENGTH TO STRENGTH   Edward Woodall Naylor (1867-1934)

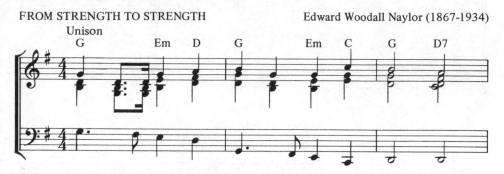

1   Soldiers of Christ, arise,
        And put your armour on,
Strong in the strength which God supplies
        Through His eternal Son;
        Strong in the Lord of Hosts,
        And in His mighty power,
Who in the strength of Jesus trusts
        Is more than conqueror.

2   Stand then in His great might,
        With all His strength endued;
But take, to arm you for the fight,
        The panoply of God;
        That, having all things done,
        And all your conflicts passed,
Ye may o'ercome through Christ alone,
        And stand entire at last.

3   Stand then against your foes,
        In close and firm array;
Legions of wily fiends oppose
        Throughout the evil day:
        But meet the sons of night;
        But mock their vain design,
Armed in the arms of heavenly light,
        Of righteousness divine.

4   Leave no unguarded place,
        No weakness of the soul;
Take every virtue, every grace,
        And fortify the whole:
        Indissolubly joined,
        To battle all proceed;
But arm yourselves with all the mind
        That was in Christ, your Head.

Charles Wesley, 1707-88

208   Soon and very soon

Andrae Crouch

Capo 1

Word Music (UK), Northbridge Road, Berkhamsted, Herts HP4 1EH.

209 Spirit of the living God

Capo 3

arr. W.G. Hathaway

1. Spi - rit of the liv - ing God, fall a - fresh on me,
Spi - rit of the liv - ing God, fall a - fresh on me:
Break me, melt me, mould me, fill me
Spi - rit of the liv - ing God, fall a - fresh on me.

210 Stand up and bless the Lord

ST. MICHAEL

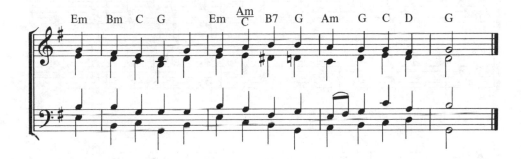

1   Stand up and bless the Lord,
      Ye people of His choice;
  Stand up and bless the Lord your God,
      With heart and soul and voice.

2   Though high above all praise,
      Above all blessing high,
  Who would not fear His holy name?
      And laud and magnify?

3   O for the living flame
      From His own altar brought,
  O touch our lips, our minds inspire,
      And wing to heaven our thought!

4   There, with benign regard,
      Our hymns He deigns to hear;
  Though unrevealed to mortal sense,
      Our spirits feel Him near.

5   God is our strength and song,
      And His salvation ours;
  Then be His love in Christ proclaimed
      With all our ransomed powers.

6   Stand up and bless the Lord,
      The Lord your God adore;
  Stand up and bless His glorious name
      Henceforth for evermore.

James Montgomery 1771-1854

211 Stand up! Stand up for Jesus

MORNING LIGHT 76.76.D

G.J. Webb (1803-87)

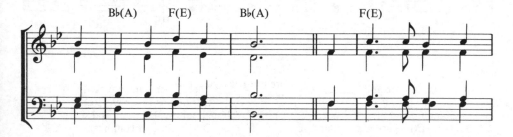

1 Stand up! stand up for Jesus!
   Ye soldiers of the cross,
   Lift high His royal banner;
   It must not suffer loss.
   From victory unto victory
   His army shall He lead,
   Till every foe is vanquished
   And Christ is Lord indeed.

2 Stand up! stand up for Jesus!
   The trumpet-call obey;
   Forth to the mighty conflict
   In this His glorious day.
   Ye that are men, now serve Him
   Against unnumbered foes;
   Let courage rise with danger,
   And strength to strength oppose.

3 Stand up! stand up for Jesus!
   Stand in His strength alone;
   The arm of flesh will fail you,
   Ye dare not trust your own.
   Put on the gospel armour,
   Each piece put on with prayer;
   Where duty calls, or danger,
   Be never wanting there.

4 Stand up! stand up for Jesus!
   The strife will not be long;
   This day the noise of battle,
   The next the victor's song.
   To him that overcometh
   A crown of life shall be;
   He with the King of glory
   Shall reign eternally.

George Duffield 1818-88

212 Take my life

NOTTINGHAM 7.7.7.7.　　　　Attributed to Wolfgang Amadeus Mozart (1756 - 91)

1. Take my life, and let it be Con - se -
2. Take my hands, and let them move At the
3. Take my voice, and let me sing Al - ways,

cra - ted, Lord, to Thee; Take my mo - ments and my
im - pulse of Thy love; Take my feet,— and let them
on - ly, for my King; Take my lips,— and let them

days, Let them flow— in cease - less praise.
be Swift and beau - ti - ful for Thee.
be Filled with mess - a - ges from Thee.

4 Take my silver and my gold,
　Not a mite would I withhold;
　Take my intellect, and use
　Every power as Thou shalt choose.

5 Take my will, and make it Thine;
　It shall be no longer mine:
　Take my heart, it is Thine own;
　It shall be Thy royal throne.

6 Take my love; my Lord, I pour
　At Thy feet its treasure store:
　Take myself, and I will be
　Ever, only, all, for Thee.

Frances Ridley Havergal
1836-79

213 Teach me to live

Elizabeth M. Dyke

1 Teach me to live day by day in your presence, Lord
  Day by day in your presence, Lord, Teach me to live

2 Teach me to praise day by day in your Spirit, Lord *etc.*

3 Teach me to love day by day in your power, Lord *etc.*

4 Teach me to give day by day from my wealth, O Lord *etc.*

214 Take time to be holy

TAKE TIME TO BE HOLY 11. 11. 11. 11. G.C. Stebbins (1846-1945)

Capo 1

1 Take time to be holy, speak oft with thy Lord;
   Abide in Him always, and feed on His Word.
   Make friends of God's children, help those who are weak;
   Forgetting in nothing His blessing to seek.

2 Take time to be holy, the world rushes on;
   Spend much time in secret with Jesus alone –
   By looking to Jesus, like Him thou shalt be!
   Thy friends in thy conduct His likeness shall see.

3 Take time to be holy, let Him be thy guide;
   And run not before Him, whatever betide;
   In joy or in sorrow still follow thy Lord,
   And, looking to Jesus, still trust in His Word.

4 Take time to be holy, be calm in thy soul;
   Each thought and each temper beneath His control;
   Thus led by His Spirit to fountains of love,
   Thou soon shalt be fitted for service above.

W.D. Longstaff 1822-94

215(i) Tell out my soul

Capo 3
T. Dudley-Smith
With a swing

M.A. Baughen

1. Tell out, my soul, the great-ness of the Lord; Un-num-bered bless - ings give my spi - rit voice; Ten - der to me the pro-mise of His Word; In God my Sa - viour shall my heart re - joice.

2 Tell out, my soul, the greatness of His Name!
  Make known His might, the deeds His arm has done;
  His mercy sure, from age to age the same;
  His Holy Name — the Lord, the Mighty One.

3 Tell out, my soul, the greatness of His might!
  Powers and dominions lay their glory by.
  Proud hearts and stubborn wills are put to flight,
  The hungry fed, the humble lifted high.

4 Tell out, my soul, the glories of His word!
  Firm is His promise, and His mercy sure,
  Tell out, my soul, the greatness of the Lord
  To children's children and for evermore!

© Timothy Dudley-Smith

215(ii)

WOODLANDS 10 10 10 10   W. Greatorex (1877-1949)

1 Tell out, my soul, the greatness of the
    Lord!
  Unnumbered blessings give my spirit
    voice;
  Tender to me the promise of His word —
  In God my Saviour shall my heart
    rejoice.

2 Tell out, my soul, the greatness of His
    name!
  Make known His might, the deeds His
    arm has done;
  His mercy sure, from age to age the
    same —
  His Holy Name: the Lord, the Mighty
    One.

3 Tell out, my soul, the greatness of His
    might!
  Powers and dominions lay their glory by.
  Proud hearts and stubborn will are put
    to flight,
  The hungry fed, the humble lifted high.

4 Tell out, my soul, the glories of His
    word!
  Firm is His promise, and His mercy sure,
  Tell out, my soul, the greatness of the
    Lord
  To children's children and for evermore!

© *Timothy Dudley-Smith*

216 Thank you Jesus

A. Huntley
arr. Roland Fudge

With strength

Capo 1 (E)

Thank you Je - sus_____ thank you

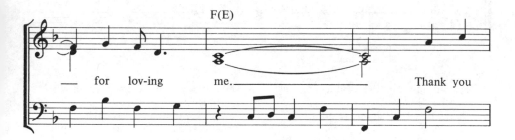

Je - sus_____ thank you Lord_____

___ for lov-ing me._____ Thank you

Je - sus,_____ thank you Je -

sus thank you Lord_____ for lov - ing

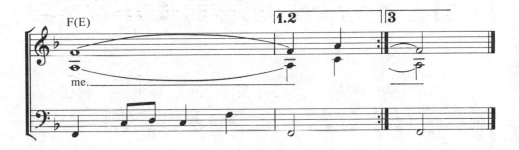

me._____

2 You went to Calvary, there you died for me,
  Thank you Lord for loving me. *(Repeat)*

3 You rose up from the grave, to me new life you gave,
  Thank you Lord for loving me. *(Repeat)*

4 You're coming back again, and we with you shall reign,
  Thank you Lord for loving me. *(Repeat)*

217 The Church's one foundation

AURELIA

S.S. Wesley (1810-76)

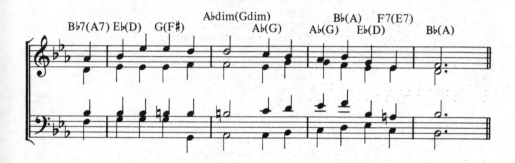

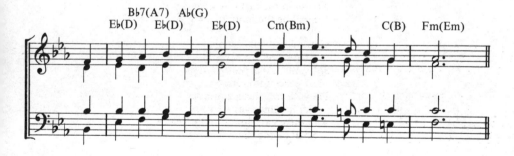

1 The Church's one foundation
   Is Jesus Christ our Lord:
She is His new creation
   By water and the word;
From heaven He came and sought her
   To be His holy bride;
With His own blood He bought her,
   And for her life He died.

2 Elect from every nation,
   Yet one o'er all the earth,
Her charter of salvation
   One Lord, one faith, one birth,
One holy name she blesses,
   Partakes one holy food,
And to one hope she presses,
   With every grace endued.

3 Though with a scornful wonder
   Men see her sore oppressed,
By schisms rent asunder,
   By heresies distressed;
Yet saints their watch are keeping,
   Their cry goes up: How long?
And soon the night of weeping
   Shall be the morn of song.

4 Mid toil and tribulation,
   And tumult of her war,
She waits the consummation
   Of peace for evermore,
Till with the vision glorious
   Her longing eyes are blest,
And the great Church victorious
   Shall be the Church at rest.

5 Yet she on earth hath union
   With God the Three in One,
And mystic sweet communion
   With those whose rest is won.
O happy ones and holy!
   Lord, give us grace that we,
Like them, the meek and lowly,
   On high may dwell with Thee.

Samuel John Stone, 1839-1900

218　The day Thou gavest

ST. CLEMENT 9.8.9.8.　　　　　　　　　　　C.C. Scholefield (1839-1904)

1 The day Thou gavest, Lord, is ended,
　The darkness falls at Thy behest;
　To Thee our morning hymns ascended,
　Thy praise shall sanctify our rest.

2 We thank Thee that Thy Church
　　unsleeping,
　While earth rolls onward into light,
　Through all the world her watch is
　　keeping,
　And rests not now by day or night.

3 As o'er each continent and island
　The dawn leads on another day,
　The voice of prayer is never silent,
　　Nor dies the strain of praise away.

4 The sun that bids us rest is waking
　Our brethren 'neath the western sky,
　And hour by hour fresh lips are making
　Thy wondrous doings heard on high.

5 So be it, Lord; Thy throne shall never,
　Like earth's proud empires, pass
　　away;
　Thy kingdom stands, and grows for
　　ever,
　Till all Thy creatures own Thy sway.

John Ellerton 1826-93

219 The greatest thing

Mark Pendergras

The great-est thing___ in all my life is know-ing you.___ The
The great-est thing___ in all my life is lov-ing you.___ The
The great-est thing___ in all my life is serv-ing you.___ The

great-est thing___ in all my life is know-ing you.___ I want to
great-est thing___ in all my life is lov-ing you.___ I want to
great-est thing___ in all my life is serv-ing you.___ I want to

know you more; I want to know you more. The
love you more; I want to love you more. The
serve you more; I want to serve you more. The

great-est thing___ in all my life is know - ing you.
great-est thing___ in all my life is lov - ing you.
great-est thing___ in all my life is serv - ing you.

220 The head that once

St. MAGNUS C.M.

J. Clark (c. 1670-1707)

1 The head that once was crowned with
    thorns
  Is crowned with glory now:
A royal diadem adorns
  The mighty victor's brow.

2 The highest place that heaven affords
  Is His by sovereign right:
The King of kings and Lord of lords,
  He reigns in perfect light.

3 The joy of all who dwell above,
  The joy of all below,
To whom He manifests His love,
  And grants His name to know.

4 To them the cross, with all its shame,
  With all its grace, is given:
Their name an everlasting name,
  Their joy the joy of heaven.

5 They suffer with their Lord below;
  They reign with Him above;
Their profit and their joy, to know
  The mystery of His love.

6 The cross He bore is life and health,
  Though shame and death to Him;
His people's hope, His people's wealth,
  Their everlasting theme.

Thomas Kelly 1769-1855

221 The King of Love

DOMINUS REGIT ME 8.7.8.7. Iambic.

J.B. Dykes (1823-76)

1 The King of love my Shepherd is,
  Whose goodness faileth never;
 I nothing lack if I am His
  And He is mine for ever.

2 Where streams of living water flow
  My ransomed soul He leadeth,
 And where the verdant pastures grow
  With food celestial feedeth.

3 Perverse and foolish oft I strayed;
  But yet in love He sought me,
 And on His shoulder gently laid,
  And home rejoicing brought me.

4 In death's dark vale I fear no ill
  With Thee, dear Lord, beside me;
 Thy rod and staff my comfort still,
  Thy Cross before to guide me.

5 Thou spread'st a table in my sight;
  Thy unction grace bestoweth;
 And O what transport of delight
  From Thy pure chalice floweth!

6 And so through all the length of days
  Thy goodness faileth never;
 Good Shepherd, may I sing Thy praise
  Within Thy House for ever!

Henry Williams Baker 1821-77

343

222 The King is among us

Graham Kendrick
Arrangement by Chris Rolinson

The king is a - mong us___

His spi - rit is here___

let's draw near and wor -

ship, let songs fill the air_____

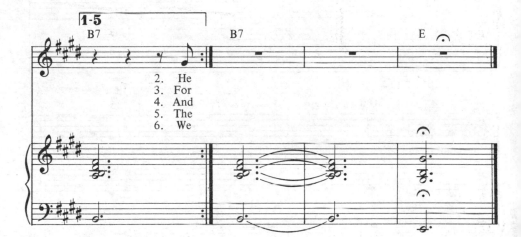

1-5

2. He
3. For
4. And
5. The
6. We

2 He looks down upon us
   Delight in his face
   Enjoying his children's love
   Enthralled by our praise

3 For each child is special
   Accepted and loved
   A love gift from Jesus
   To his Father above

4 And now he is giving
   His gifts to us all
   For no one is worthless
   And each one is called

5 The Spirit's anointing
   On all flesh comes down
   And we shall be channels
   For works like his own

6 We come now believing
   Your promise of power
   For we are your people
   And this is your hour

Graham Kendrick

345

223 The light of Christ

Flowing

Donald Fishel
Arr. Betty Pulkingham

VERSES

1. All men must be born a - gain to see the king - dom of
2. God gave up his on - ly Son out of love for the
3. The light of God has come to us so that we might have sal -

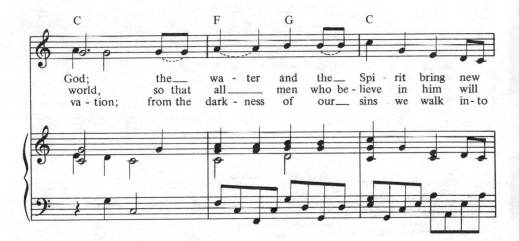

God; the wa - ter and the Spi - rit bring new
world, so that all men who be - lieve in him will
va - tion; from the dark - ness of our sins we walk in - to

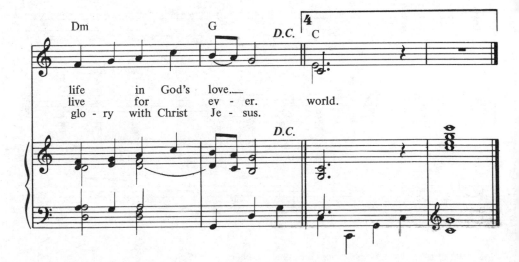

life in God's love.
live for ev - er. world.
glo - ry with Christ Je - sus.

D.C.

347

224 The Lord is a great and mighty King

Diane Davis

The Lord is a great and might-y king,

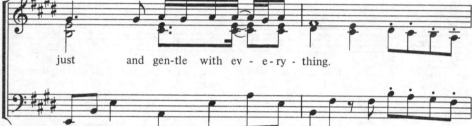

just and gen-tle with ev - e - ry - thing.

So with hap-pi-ness___ we sing,

and let his prais-es ring. ring.___

1. We are his voice,__ we his song;
2. We are his bo - dy here on earth;
3. For our Lord__ we will stand,
4. The Lord our God__ is one,

let us praise him all day long.
from a - bove he gave us birth.
sent by him to ev - 'ry land.
Fa - ther, Spi - rit and the Son.

Al - le - lu - ia!__ The

225 The Lord is my strength

Roland Fudge

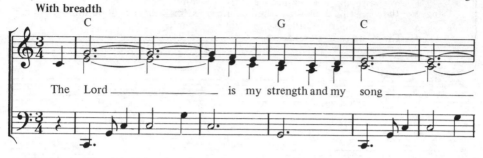

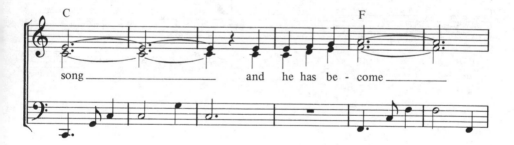

Sing to the Lord _____ for he has done mar-vel-lous

things _____ Sing to the Lord _____

____ for he has done mar-vel-lous things _____

Sing to the Lord _____ Sing to the

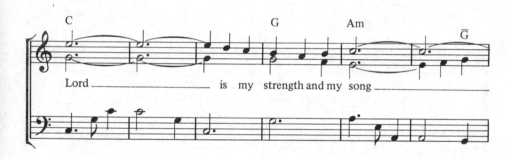

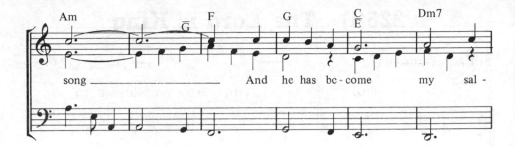

song _____ And he has be-come my sal-

va - tion. _____

The Lord is my strength and my song,
The Lord is my strength and my song,
And he has become my salvation.
Sing to the Lord, for he has done marvellous things
Sing to the Lord, for he has done marvellous things
Sing to the Lord, sing to the Lord,
Sing to the Lord, for he has done marvellous things.
The Lord is my strength and my song,
The Lord is my strength and my song,
And he has become my salvation.

226(i) The Lord is King

CHURCH TRIUMPHANT

J.W. Elliott (1833-1915)

Capo 3

226(ii)

NIAGARA L.M.

R. Jackson (1840-1914)

1 The Lord is King! lift up thy voice,
   O earth, and all ye heavens rejoice;
   From world to world the joy shall ring:
   "The Lord omnipotent is King!"

2 The Lord is King! who then shall dare
   Resist His will, distrust His care,
   Or murmur at His wise decrees,
   Or doubt His royal promises?

3 The Lord is King! child of the dust,
   The judge of all the earth is just;
   Holy and true are all His ways:
   Let every creature speak His praise.

4 He reigns! ye saints, exalt your strains;
   Your God is King, your Father reigns:
   And He is at the Father's side,
   The man of love, the crucified.

5 One Lord, one empire, all secures;
   He reigns, — and life and death are
         yours,
   Through earth and heaven one song
         shall ring,
   "The Lord omnipotent is King!"

Josiah Conder, 1789-1855

227 The Lord's my Shepherd

CRIMOND C.M.

Capo 3

Melody by
Jessie S. Irvine (1836-87)

1 The Lord's my shepherd, I'll not want;
   He makes me down to lie
In pastures green; He leadeth me
   The quiet waters by.

2 My soul He doth restore again,
   And me to walk doth make
Within the paths of righteousness,
   E'en for His own name's sake.

3 Yea, though I walk through death's
     dark vale,
   Yet will I fear none ill;
For Thou art with me, and Thy rod
   And staff me comfort still.

4 My table Thou hast furnishèd
   In presence of my foes;
My head Thou dost with oil anoint,
   And my cup overflows.

5 Goodness and mercy all my life
   Shall surely follow me;
And in God's house for evermore
   My dwelling-place shall be.

Francis Rous, 1579-1659
revised for Scottish Psalter, 1650

228 Therefore we lift our hearts

Colin Green
Arr. Norman Warren

1. There - fore we   lift   our hearts in   praise, Sing   to the
2. There for   ev - 'ry - one to   see,   There on the
3. There for   sad   and bro - ken men   He   rose up
4. There for   such great pain and cost The   Spi - rit
5. There - fore we   lift   our hearts in   praise, Sing   to the

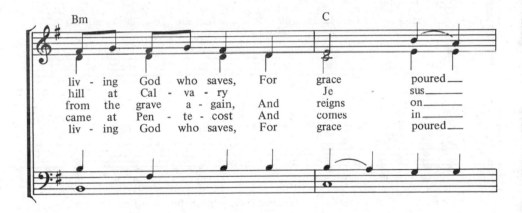

liv - ing God who saves, For   grace   poured___
hill   at   Cal - va - ry   Je - sus___
from the grave a - gain, And   reigns on___
came at   Pen - te - cost   And   comes   in___
liv - ing God who saves, For   grace   poured___

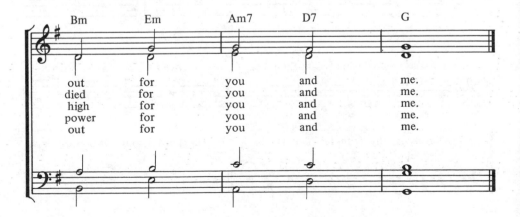

out   for   you   and   me.
died   for   you   and   me.
high   for   you   and   me.
power for   you   and   me.
out   for   you   and   me.

© This arrangement Norman Warren, 1980

357

229 The steadfast love

Capo 4 (C)

Edith McNeill

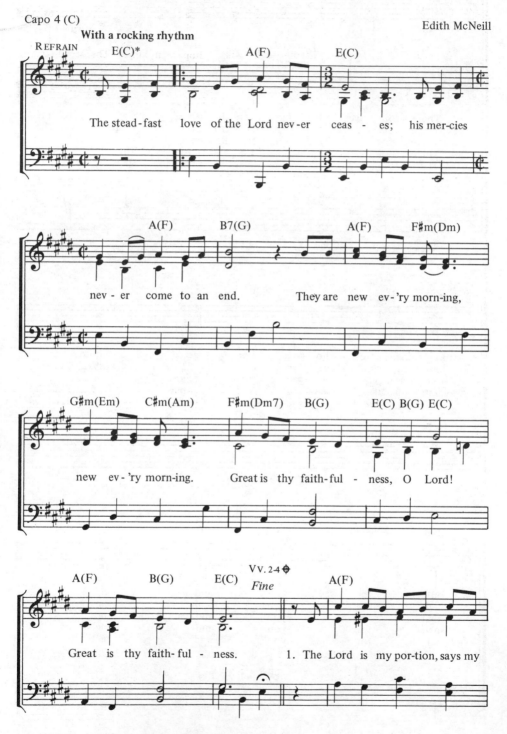

The stead-fast love of the Lord nev-er ceas - es; his mer-cies nev - er come to an end. They are new ev-'ry morn-ing, new ev-'ry morn-ing. Great is thy faith-ful - ness, O Lord! Great is thy faith-ful - ness. 1. The Lord is my por-tion, says my

G#m(Em)   A(F)   F#m(Dm) B7(G7)   E(C)

soul.   There-fore I will   hope in him. The stead-fast

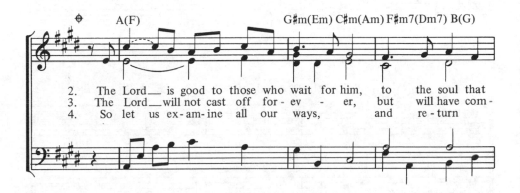

A(F)   G#m(Em) C#m(Am) F#m7(Dm7) B(G)

2. The Lord—is good to those who wait for him, to the soul that
3. The Lord—will not cast off for-ev-er, but will have com-
4. So let us ex-am-ine all our ways, and re-turn

E(C)   A(F)   G#m(Em) C#m(Am)

seeks him. It is good—that we should wait qui-et-ly—
pas-sion. For—he does not will-ing-ly af-flict or
to the Lord. Let us lift up our hearts and hands

F#(D)   F#7(D7)   B(G)   B7(G7) E(C)

for the sal-va-tion of the Lord.
grieve the— sons— of— men.
to— God— in— heav'n.

The stead-fast

* Guitar chords and piano arrangement not designed to be used together.

230 There is a green hill

HORSLEY C.M.

W. Horsley (1774-1858)

Capo 1

1 There is a green hill far away,
　　Without a city wall,
　Where the dear Lord was crucified
　　Who died to save us all.

2 We may not know, we cannot tell
　　What pains He had to bear;
　But we believe it was for us
　　He hung and suffered there.

3 He died that we might be forgiven,
　　He died to make us good,
　That we might go at last to heaven
　　Saved by His precious blood.

4 There was no other good enough
　　To pay the price of sin;
　He only could unlock the gate
　　Of heaven, and let us in.

5 O dearly, dearly has He loved,
　　And we must love Him too,
　And trust in His redeeming blood,
　　And try His works to do.

Cecil Frances Alexander, 1823-95

231 There is none holy as the Lord

1 SAMUEL 2:2

Gary Garrett

Not too slowly

There is none ho-ly as the Lord.

There is none be - side Thee.

Nei - ther is there an - y rock like our God.

There is none ho - ly as the Lord.

232 There is a Name

F. Whitfield

W.H. Rudd

1. There is a Name I love to hear, I love to
speak its worth; It sounds like music
in my ear, The sweet-est name on earth.

2. It tells me of a Sav-iour's love, Who died to
set me free; It tells me of His
prec-ious blood, The sin-ner's per-fect plea.

3. It tells of One whose lov-ing heart Can feel my
deep-est woe, Who in my sor-row
bears a part That none can bear be-low.

4. It bids my trem-bling heart re-joice, It dries each
ris-ing tear; It tells me in a
"still, small voice" To trust and nev-er fear.

5. Je-sus, the Name I love so well, The Name I
love to hear! No saint on earth its
worth can tell, No heart con-ceive how dear!

233 There's a quiet understanding

Tedd Smith

Tedd Smith

1. There's a qui-et un-der-stand-ing___ when we're gath-ered in the Spi - rit,___ It's a pro-mise that He gives us,___ when we gath-er in His name. There's a love we feel in Je-sus,___ there's a man-na that He feeds us,___ It's a pro-mise that He gives us___ When we gath-er in His name.

2. And we know when we're to-geth-er,___ shar-ing love and un-der-stand-ing,___ That our broth-ers and our sis-ters___ feel the one-ness that He brings. Thank You, thank You, thank You, Je-sus,___ for the way You love and feed us,___ For the man-y ways You lead us___ Thank You, thank You, Lord.

Repeat ad lib.

234 There's a way back

E.H.S.

E.H. Swinstead

There's a way back to God from the dark paths of sin; There's a
door that is o-pen and you may go in: At Cal-va-ry's cross is
where you be-gin, When you come as a sin-ner to Je - sus.

235 There's a sound

BATTLE HYMN

Graham Kendrick

1. There's a sound on the wind like a vic-to-ry

song, lis-ten now, let it rest on your soul.

It's a song that I learned from a

hea-ven-ly King, It's a song of a

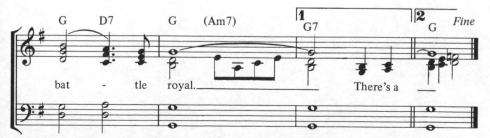

bat-tle royal. There's a

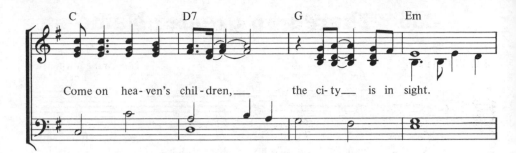

Come on hea-ven's chil-dren,___ the ci-ty___ is in sight.

There will be___ no sad-ness on the oth-er side.

2 There's a loud shout of victory that leaps from our hearts
As we wait for our conquering King.
There's a triumph resounding from dark ages past
To the victory song we now sing.

3 There'll be crowns for the conquerors and white robes to wear,
There will be no more sorrow or pain.
And the battles of earth shall be lost in the sight
Of the glorious Lamb that was slain.

4 Now the king of the ages approaches the earth,
He will burst through the gates of the sky.
And all men shall bow down to his beautiful name;
We shall rise with a shout, we shall fly!

Sequence: Verse 1, Verse 2, Chorus, Verse 3, Verse 4, Chorus,
Repeat Verse 4.

236 There's no greater Name

M.A. Baughen

M.A. Baughen

There's no great-er name than Je - sus, Name of him who
In our minds by faith pro - fes - sing, In our hearts by

came to save us In that sa - ving name of Je - sus eve - ry
in - ward bless - ing, On our tongues by words con - fess - ing, Je - sus

1 knee should bow.___ 2 Christ is Lord.___ Let eve-ry thing that is

'neath the ground, Let eve-ry - thing in the world a - round, Let eve-ry-

thing that's high o'er the sky___ Bow at Je - sus' Name.___

D.C. al Fine (and 2nd Time bar)

237 Thou didst leave thy throne

MARGARET Irregular

T.R. Matthews (1826-1910)

1   Thou didst leave Thy throne
        And Thy kingly crown,
When Thou camest to earth for me;
        But in Bethlehem's home
        Was there found no room
For Thy holy nativity:
        O come to my heart, Lord Jesus;
There is room in my heart for Thee.

2   Heaven's arches rang
        When the angels sang,
Proclaiming Thy royal degree;
        But of lowly birth
        Cam'st Thou, Lord, on earth,
And in great humility:
        O come to my heart, Lord Jesus;
There is room in my heart for Thee.

3   The foxes found rest,
        And the birds their nest,
In the shade of the cedar-tree;
        But Thy couch was the sod,
        O Thou Son of God,
In the deserts of Galilee;
        O come to my heart, Lord Jesus,
There is room in my heart for Thee.

4   Thou camest, O Lord,
        With the living word
That should set Thy people free;
        But, with mocking scorn
        And with crown of thorn,
They bore Thee to Calvary:
        O come to my heart, Lord Jesus;
Thy Cross is my only plea.

5   When heaven's arches ring,
        And her choirs shall sing,
At Thy coming to victory,
        Let Thy voice call me home,
        Saying: Yet there is room,
There is room at My side for thee!
        And my heart shall rejoice, Lord
            Jesus,
When Thou comest and callest for me.

Emily Elizabeth Steele Elliott,
1836-97

369

238 Thine be the glory

MACCABAEUS 10.11.11.11 with Refrain

G.F. Handel (1685-1759)

Thine be the glory

1 Thine be the glory, risen, conquering Son,
  Endless is the victory Thou o'er death hast won;
  Angels in bright raiment rolled the stone away,
  Kept the folded grave-clothes, where Thy body lay.

  Thine be the glory, risen, conquering Son,
  Endless is the victory Thou o'er death hast won.

2 Lo! Jesus meets us, risen from the tomb;
  Lovingly He greets us, scatters fear and gloom;
  Let the Church with gladness hymns of triumph sing,
  For her Lord now liveth; death hath lost its sting.

  Thine be the glory, risen, conquering Son,
  Endless is the victory Thou o'er death hast won.

3 No more we doubt Thee, glorious Prince of life;
  Life is nought without Thee: aid us in our strife;
  Make us more than conquerors, through Thy deathless love:
  Bring us safe through Jordan to Thy home above.

  Thine be the glory, risen, conquering Son,
  Endless is the victory Tho o'er death hast won.

> *Edmond Budry, 1854-1932*
> *tr. R. Birch Hoyle, 1875-1939*

239 This is the day

Fiji Island Folk Melody
arr. Roland Fudge

1. This is the day, this is the day that the Lord has made, that the Lord has made.
2. This is the day, this is the day when he rose again, when he rose again.
3. This is the day, this is the day when the Spirit came, when the Spirit came.

We will re-joice, we will re-joice and be glad in it, and be glad in it.

Published by Hodder and Stoughton — Sounds of Living Water.

This is is   the day   that the   Lord   has   made.
This is is   the day   when he   rose   a -   gain.
This is is   the day   when the   Spi - rit   came.

We will   re-joice   and be   glad   in   it.

This is   the day,   this is   the day   that the
This is   the day,   this is   the day   when he
This is   the day,   this is   the day   when the

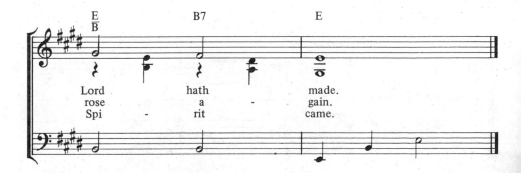

Lord   hath   made.
rose   a -   gain.
Spi -   rit   came.

373

240 Thou art my God

Psalm 118:28,29.

Tony Hopkins
arr. Roland Fudge

Rich and broad

Thou art my God and I will praise Thee.

Thou art my God I will ex -

alt ___ Thee. ___ O give thanks un-to the

Lord for He is good, ___ For His

mer - cy en - dur - eth for ev - er.

241 Thy loving kindness

author unknown
Arr. Margaret Evans

Happily

1. Thy lov-ing kind - ness___ is bet-ter than life,___ Thy lov-ing
2. I lift my hands up___ un-to Thy name,___ I lift my

kind - ness___ is bet-ter than life.___ {My lips shall praise Thee,_thus will I
hands up___ un-to Thy name.___

bless Thee,___ Thy lov-ing kind-ness is bet-ter than life.___

242 Thou art worthy

Rev. 4: II and 5. 9.10.
Verse 2 — Tom Smail

Pauline Michael Mills

Capo 1

376

243 Thou, Lord, hast given thyself

SPRINGFIELD 11.10.11.10 Dactylic

H.J. Gauntlett (1805-76)

Capo 1

1 Thou, Lord, hast given Thyself for our healing;
    Poured out Thy life that our souls might be freed.
 Love, from the heart of the Father, revealing
    Light for our darkness and grace for our need.

2 Saviour of men, our humanity sharing
    Give us a passion for souls that are lost.
 Help us to follow, Thy gospel declaring;
    Daily to serve Thee and count not the cost.

3 Pray we for men who today in their blindness
    Wander from Thee and Thy kingdom of truth:
 Grant them a sight of Thy great loving-kindness,
    Lord of their manhood and guide of their youth.

4 Come, Holy Spirit, to cleanse and renew us:
    Purge us from evil and fill us with power:
 Thus shall the waters of healing flow through us;
    So shall revival be born in this hour.

5 Give to Thy Church, as she tells forth the story,
    Strength for her weakness and trust for her fears;
 Make her a channel of grace for Thy glory,
    Answer her prayers in the midst of the years.

R.D. Browne, 1905-

244 Thou, whose almighty word

MOSCOW

Felice de Giardini (1716-96)

1. Thou, Whose al-migh-ty word Cha-os and dark-ness heard,
2. Thou, Who didst come to bring, On Thy re-deem-ing wing,
3. Spi-rit of truth and love, Life giv-ing, ho-ly Dove,

And took their flight; Hear us, we hum-bly pray, And where the
Heal-ing and sight, Health to the sick in mind, Sight to the
Speed forth Thy flight; Move on the wa-ters' face, Bear-ing the

Gos-pel day Sheds not its glo-rious ray, Let there be light.
in-ly blind; O now to all—man-kind Let there be light.
lamp of grace, And in earth's dark-est place Let there be light.

4 Blessèd and holy Three,
Glorious Trinity,
   Wisdom, love, might;
Boundless as ocean's tide
Rolling in fullest pride,
Through the earth, far and wide,
   Let there be light.

John Marriott, 1780-1825

379

245 Thou wilt keep him

Anon.
Arr. Paul Beckwith

Quietly

1. Thou_ wilt keep him in per - fect peace, Thou_ wilt keep him in
2. Mar - vel not that I say un - to you, Mar - vel not that I
3. Though your sins as scar - let be, Though your sins as

per - fect peace, Thou_ wilt keep him in
say un - to you, Mar - vel not that I
scar - let be, Though_ your sins as

per - fect peace Whose mind is stayed on thee.____
say un - to you, Ye must be born a - gain.____
scar - let be, They shall be white as snow.____

4 If the Son shall make you free,
If the Son shall make you free,
If the Son shall make you free,
Ye shall be free indeed.

5 They that wait upon the Lord,
They that wait upon the Lord,
They that wait upon the Lord,
They shall renew their strength.

6 Whom shall I send and who will go?
Whom shall I send and who will go?
Whom shall I send and who will go?
Here I am, Lord, send me.

246 Through all the changing scenes

WILTSHIRE C.M.
Capo 1 (A)

G.T. Smart (1776-1867)

1 Through all the changing scenes of life,
  In trouble and in joy,
  The praises of my God shall still
  My heart and tongue employ.

2 Of His deliverance I will boast,
  Till all that are distressed
  From my example comfort take,
  And charm their griefs to rest.

3 O magnify the Lord with me,
  With me exalt His name;
  When in distress to Him I called,
  He to my rescue came.

4 The hosts of God encamp around
  The dwellings of the just;
  Deliverance He affords to all
  Who on His succour trust.

5 O make but trial of His love;
  Experience will decide
  How blest they are, and only they,
  Who in His truth confide.

6 Fear Him, ye saints, and you will then
  Have nothing else to fear;
  Make you His service your delight,
  He'll make your wants His care.

Nahum Tate, 1652-1715
Nicholas Brady, 1639-1726

381

247 Thy hand, O God

THORNBURY 76.76.D
Capo 2

Basil Harwood (1859-1949)

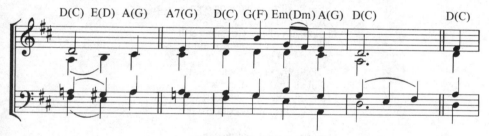

1 Thy hand, O God, has guided
   Thy flock from age to age;
The wondrous tale is written,
   Full clear, on every page;
Our fathers owned Thy goodness,
   And we their deeds record;
And both of this bear witness,
   One Church, one Faith, one Lord.

2 Thy heralds brought glad tidings
   To greatest, as to least;
They bade men rise, and hasten
   To share the great King's feast;
And this was all their teaching,
   In every deed and word,
To all alike proclaiming
   One Church, one Faith, one Lord.

3 Through many a day of darkness,
   Through many a scene of strife,
The faithful few fought bravely
   To guard the nation's life.
Their gospel of redemption,
   Sin pardoned, man restored,
Was all in this enfolded,
   One Church, one Faith, one Lord.

4 Thy mercy will not fail us,
   Nor leave Thy work undone;
With Thy right hand to help us,
   The victory shall be won;
And then, by men and angels,
   Thy name shall be adored,
And this shall be their anthem,
   One Church, one Faith, one Lord.

E.H. Plumptre 1821-91

248 To God be the glory!

W.H. Doane (1832-1915)

1 To God be the glory! Great things He hath done!
   So loved He the world that He gave us His Son;
   Who yielded His life an atonement for sin,
   And opened the life gate that all may go in.
      Praise the Lord! Praise the Lord! Let the earth hear His voice!
      Praise the Lord! Praise the Lord! Let the people rejoice!
      O come to the Father, through Jesus the Son:
      And give Him the glory! Great things He hath done!

2 O perfect redemption, the purchase of blood!
   To every believer the promise of God;
   The vilest offender who truly believes,
   That moment from Jesus a pardon receives.

3 Great things He hath taught us, great things He hath done,
   And great our rejoicing through Jesus the Son;
   But purer, and higher, and greater will be
   Our wonder, our rapture, when Jesus we see.

Frances van Alstyne 1820-1915

249 Turn your eyes upon Jesus

Capo 3(D)

Helen H. Lemmel

1. O soul, are you wea-ry and trou-bled? No light in the
2. Thro' death in-to life ev-er-last-ing He passed, and we
3. His word shall not fail you He prom-ised; Be-lieve Him, and

dark-ness you see?___ There's light for a look at the Sav-
fol-low Him there;___ Ov-er us sin no more hath do-min-
all will be well: Then go to a world that is dy-

iour, And life more a-bun-dant and free!)
ion For more than con-qu'rors we are!
ing, His per-fect sal-va-tion to tell!)

Turn your eyes up-on Je-sus, Look full in His

won-der-ful face;_____ And the things of earth will grow strange-ly dim In the light of His glo-ry and grace._____

250 Timeless love!

Psalm 89:1 – 18
Timothy Dudley-Smith

Norman Warren

Time-less love! We sing the sto - ry, Praise His won - ders, tell His
By His faith - ful-ness sur - round-ed, North and South His hand pro -
Truth and right - eous-ness en - throne Him, Just and e - qual are His

worth; Love more fair than hea-ven's glo - ry, Love more
claim; Earth and hea - ven formed and found - ed, Skies and
ways; More than hap - py, those who own Him, More than

firm than an-cient earth! Tell His faith - ful-ness a -
seas, de-clare His Name! Wind and storm o - bey His
joy, their songs of praise! Sun and Shield and great Re -

broad, Who is like Him? Praise the Lord!
word, Who is like Him? Praise the Lord!
ward, Who is like Him? Praise the Lord!

251 We are gathering

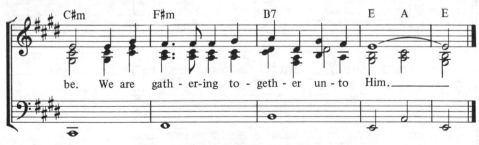

2 We are offering together unto Him. . . .

3 We are singing together unto Him. . . .

4 We are praying together unto Him. . . .

Words and Music: Anonymous

252 Victory is on our lips

Diane Fung
arr. Roland Fudge

Vic - to - ry_____ is on our lips and

in our__ lives_____ , for Je - sus____

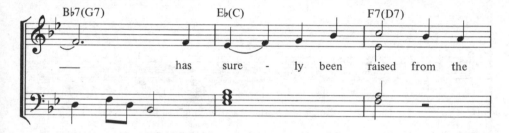

__ has sure - ly been raised from the

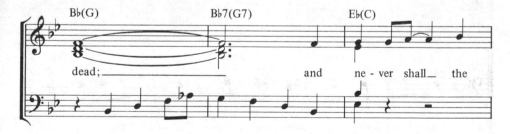

dead;_____ and ne - ver shall__ the

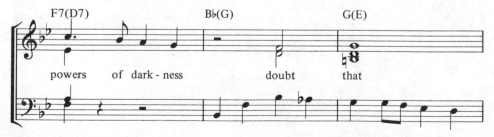

powers of dark - ness doubt that

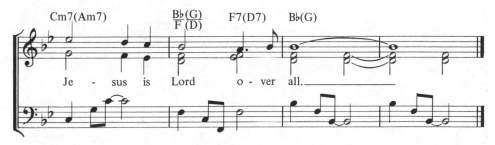

253   We have come into His house

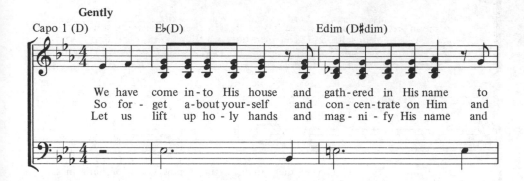

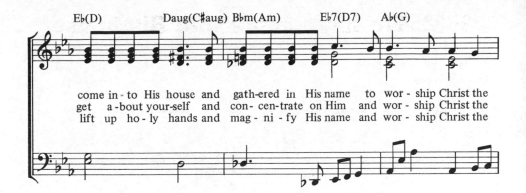

come in - to His house and gath-ered in His name to wor - ship Christ the
get a -bout your-self and con - cen-trate on Him and wor - ship Christ the
lift up ho - ly hands and mag - ni - fy His name and wor - ship Christ the

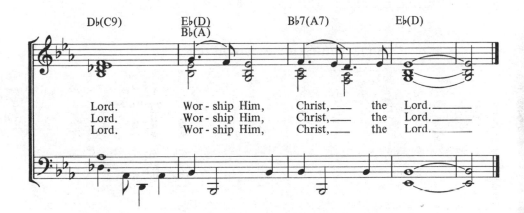

Lord.   Wor - ship Him,   Christ,___ the   Lord.___
Lord.   Wor - ship Him,   Christ,___ the   Lord.___
Lord.   Wor - ship Him,   Christ,___ the   Lord.___

254

Song omitted for copyright reasons.

255 We have heard

LIMPSFIELD 73.73.77.73

Josiah Booth (1852-1929)

1 We have heard a joyful sound:
   Jesus saves!
Spread the gladness all around:
   Jesus saves!
Bear the news to every land,
Climb the steeps and cross the waves;
Onward! 'tis our Lord's command:
   Jesus saves!

2 Sing above the battle's strife:
   Jesus saves!
By His death and endless life,
   Jesus saves!
Sing it softly through the gloom,
When the heart for mercy craves;

Sing in triumph o'er the tomb:
   Jesus saves!

3 Give the winds a mighty voice:
   Jesus saves!
Let the nations now rejoice:
   Jesus saves!
Shout salvation full and free
To every strand that ocean laves —
This our song of victory:
   Jesus saves!

Priscilla Owens 1829-1907

256 We really want to thank You

With a swing

Ed Baggett
Arr. Betty Pulkingham

We real - ly want to thank you, Lord.__
We real - ly want to bless your name.__

Hal - le - lu - jah! Je - sus is__ our king!_____

1. We thank you, Lord, for your
2. We thank you, Lord, for our
3. Praise God from whom all

gift to us, your life so rich be - yond com - pare, the
life to-geth - er, to live and move in the love of Christ, Your
bless - ings flow, Praise Him all crea - tures here be - low

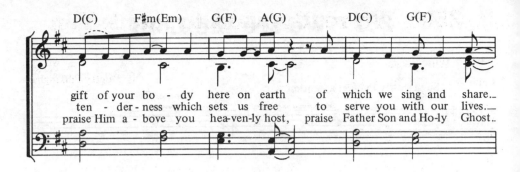

D(C)   F♯m(Em)   G(F)   A(G)   D(C)   G(F)

gift of your bo - dy here on earth   of which we sing and share...
ten - der - ness which sets us free   to serve you with our lives...
praise Him a - bove you hea-ven-ly host, praise Father Son and Ho-ly Ghost...

A(G)   REFRAIN⊕ D(C)   G(F)   D(C)

king!

257 We see the Lord

Isaiah 6:1

Anon.
Arr. Betty Pulkingham

Sung slowly in quiet adoration

We see Je - sus.

We see the Lord,

We see Je - sus.

We see the Lord, And he is

High,_____ he is high,_____

high and lift - ed up, And his train fills the tem - ple. He is

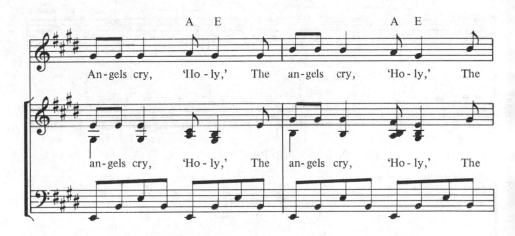

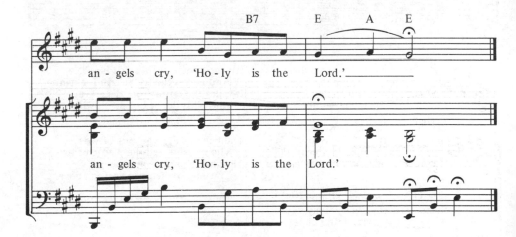

258 We sing the praise

WARRINGTON L.M.   R. Harrison (1748-1810)

1 We sing the praise of Him who died,
    Of Him who died upon the cross;
  The sinner's hope let men deride,
    For this we count the world but loss.

2 Inscribed upon the cross we see,
    In shining letters, "God is love";
  He bears our sins upon the tree,
    He brings us mercy from above.

3 The cross! it takes our guilt away,
    It holds the fainting spirit up;
  It cheers with hope the gloomy day,
    And sweetens every bitter cup.

4 It makes the coward spirit brave,
    And nerves the feeble arm for fight;
  It takes the terror from the grave,
    And gilds the bed of death with
        light.

5 The balm of life, the cure of woe,
    The measure and the pledge of love;
  The sinner's refuge here below,
    The angels' theme in heaven above.

Thomas Kelly 1769-1855

259 We will sing of our Redeemer

Words and Music by
Gordon Brattle

We will sing of our Re-deem-er, He's our King:___

All His glo-ry all His praise to you we bring;___

With our hearts and with our voi-ces Him we sing,___

We love the Lord, we love His Word. He's our King.___

401

260   We'll sing a new song

Diane Fung

Diane Fung

Lively

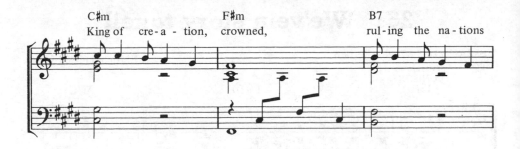

King of cre-a - tion, crowned, rul-ing the na-tions

now. _____ now. _____

261   We've a story to tell

MESSAGE 10.8.87 with Refrain
Capo 1

H.E. Nichol (1862-1926)

1 We've a story to tell to the nations,
    That shall turn their hearts to the right,
A story of truth and sweetness,
    A story of peace and light:

For the darkness shall turn to dawning,
*   And the dawning to noon-day bright,*
And Christ's great kingdom shall come on earth,
*   The kingdom of love and light.*

2 We've a song to be sung to the nations,
    That shall lift their hearts to the Lord;
A song that shall conquer evil,
    And shatter the spear and sword:
For the darkness shall turn to dawning,

3 We've a message to give to the nations,
    That the Lord who reigneth above
Hath sent us His Son to save us,
    And show us that God is love:
For the darkness shall turn to dawning,

4 We've a Saviour to show to the nations,
    Who the path of sorrow has trod,
That all of the world's great peoples
    Might come to the truth of God:
For the darkness shall turn to dawning,

Colin Sterne, 1862-1926

262　What a friend we have in Jesus

CONVERSE 87.87.D

C.C. Converse (1832-1918)

Capo 1

1 What a friend we have in Jesus,
    All our sins and griefs to bear!
What a privilege to carry
    Everything to God in prayer!
O what peace we often forfeit,
    O what needless pain we bear —
All because we do not carry
    Everything to God in prayer!

2 Have we trials and temptations?
    Is there trouble anywhere?
We should never be discouraged:
    Take it to the Lord in prayer!
Can we find a friend so faithful,
    Who will all our sorrows share?
Jesus knows our every weakness —
    Take it to the Lord in prayer!

3 Are we weak and heavy-laden,
    Cumbered with a load of care?
Jesus only is our refuge,
    Take it to the Lord in prayer!
Do thy friends despise, forsake thee?
    Take it to the Lord in prayer!
In His arms He'll take and shield thee,
    Thou wilt find a solace there.

Joseph Scriven, 1819-86

263 What a wonderful change

Rufus H. McDaniel
Capo 1(G)

Charles H. Gabriel

1. What a won-der-ful change in my life has been wrought
2. I'm pos-sessed of a hope that is stead-fast and sure,
3. There's a light in the val-ley of death now for me,
4. I shall go there to dwell in that cit-y, I know,

Since Je-sus came in-to my heart! I have light in my soul
Since Je-sus came in-to my heart! And no dark clouds of doubt
Since Je-sus came in-to my heart! And the gates of the cit-
Since Je-sus came in-to my heart! And I'm hap-py, so hap-

for which long I had sought, Since Je-sus came in-to my heart!
now my path-way ob-scure, Since Je-sus came in-to my heart!
y be-yond I can see, Since Je-sus came in-to my heart!
py, as on-ward I go, Since Je-sus came in-to my heart!

Since Je-sus came in-to my heart, Since
Since Je-sus came in, came in-to my heart, Since

Je-sus came in-to my heart, Floods of joy o'er my
Je-sus came in, came in-to my heart,

soul like the sea bil-lows roll, Since Je-sus came in-to my heart.

409

264　When I feel the touch

Keri Jones/Dave Matthews

Worshipfully

When I feel the touch___ of Your hand up-on my

life,___ it caus-es me to sing a song that I

love You, Lord. So from deep with-

in___ my spi-rit sing-eth un-to Thee,___ You are my

King, You are my God, and I love You, Lord.

265 When I survey

ROCKINGHAM L.M.
Capo 1

E. Miller (1731-1807)

1 When I survey the wondrous cross
   On which the Prince of Glory died,
My richest gain I count but loss,
   And pour contempt on all my pride.

2 Forbid it, Lord, that I should boast,
   Save in the death of Christ my God:
All the vain things that charm me most,
   I sacrifice them to His blood.

3 See from His head, His hands, His feet,
   Sorrow and love flow mingled down:
Did e'er such love and sorrow meet,
   Or thorns compose so rich a crown?

4 Were the whole realm of nature mine,
   That were an offering far too small,
Love so amazing, so divine,
   Demands my soul, my life, my all.

Isaac Watts, 1674-1748

266 When morning gilds the skies

LAUDES DOMINI 6 6.6. D.

J. Barnby (1838-96)

1 When morning gilds the skies,
  My heart awaking cries:
    May Jesus Christ be praised!
  Alike at work and prayer
  To Jesus I repair;
    May Jesus Christ be praised!

2 Does sadness fill my mind?
  A solace here I find —
    May Jesus Christ be praised!
  When evil thoughts molest,
  With this I shield my breast —
    May Jesus Christ be praised!

3 Be this, when day is past,
  Of all my thoughts the last,
    May Jesus Christ be praised!
  The night becomes as day,
  When from the heart we say:
    May Jesus Christ be praised!

4 To God, the Word, on high
  The hosts of angels cry,
    May Jesus Christ be praised!
  Let mortals, too, upraise
  Their voice in hymns of praise:
    May Jesus Christ be praised!

5 Let earth's wide circle round
  In joyful notes resound:
    May Jesus Christ be praised!
  Let air, and sea, and sky,
  From depth to height, reply:
    May Jesus Christ be praised!

6 Be this while life is mine,
  My canticle divine,
    May Jesus Christ be praised!
  Be this the eternal song
  Through all the ages long,
    May Jesus Christ be praised!

Anonymous;
tr. by Edward Caswall, 1814-78

412

267 Wherever I am

Unknown
arr. David Peacock

Quite Fast

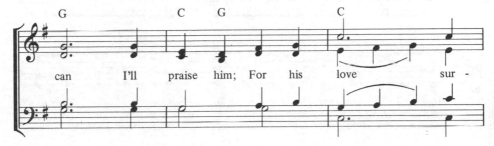

Wher - e - ver I am I'll praise him, when - e - ver I

can I'll praise him; For his love sur -

rounds me like a sea;_____ I'll praise the name of

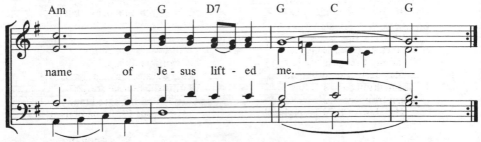

Je - sus, lift up the name of Je - sus, For the

name of Je - sus lift - ed me._____

268 When the trumpet of the Lord

ROLL CALL

James M. Black (1893 -)

1. When the trum-pet of the Lord shall sound, and
   time shall be no more, And the morn-ing breaks, e-ter-nal, bright, and
   fair; When the saved of earth shall gath-er ov-er
   on the oth-er shore,

2. On that bright and cloud-less morn-ing when the
   dead in Christ shall rise, And the glo-ry of his res-ur-rec-tion
   share; When his cho-sen ones shall gath-er to their
   home be-yond the skies,

3. Let us la-bour for the Mas-ter from the
   dawn till set-ting sun, Let us talk of all his won-d'rous love and
   care; Then when all of life is ov-er, and our
   work on earth is done,

And the roll is called up yon-der, I'll be there.

When the roll＿＿＿＿ is called up yon ＿ der, When the

When the roll is called up yon-der, I'll be there,

roll＿＿＿＿ is called up yon der, When the

When the roll is called up yon - der, I'll be there,

roll＿＿＿＿ is called up yon - der, When the

When the roll is called up yon - der, When the

roll is called up yon - der, I'll be there.

269 · When we walk with the Lord

TRUST AND OBEY 6 6.9. D. and refrain

D.B. Towner (1833-96)

1 When we walk with the Lord
   In the light of His Word
What a glory He sheds on our way!
   While we do His good will,
   He abides with us still,
And with all who will trust and obey.

  Trust and obey, for there's no other way
   To be happy in Jesus,
   But to trust and obey.

2 Not a shadow can rise,
   Not a cloud in the skies,
But His smile quickly drives it away;
   Not a doubt nor a fear,
   Not a sigh nor a tear,
Can abide while we trust and obey.

  Trust and obey. . . .

3 Not a burden we bear,
   Not a sorrow we share,
But our toil He doth richly repay;
   Not a grief nor a loss,
   Not a frown nor a cross,
But is blest if we trust and obey.

  Trust and obey. . . .

4 But we never can prove
   The delights of His love
Until all on the altar we lay;
   For the favour He shows,
   And the joy He bestows,
Are for them who will trust and obey.

  Trust and obey. . . .

5 Then in fellowship sweet
   We will sit at His feet,
Or we'll walk by His side in the way;
   What He says we will do,
   Where He sends we will go —
Never fear, only trust and obey.

  Trust and obey. . . .

  John Henry Sammis, 1846-1919

270 Who can cheer the heart

ALL THAT THRILLS MY SOUL

Words and Music Thoro Harris

Capo 3

1. Who can cheer the heart like Jesus, By His presence all divine?
2. Love of Christ so freely given, Grace of God beyond degree,
3. What a wonderful redemption! Never can a mortal know
4. Ev-'ry need His hand supplying, Ev-'ry good in Him I see;
5. By the crystal flowing river With the ransomed I will sing,

True and tender, pure and precious, O how blest to call Him mine!
Mercy higher than the heaven, Deeper than the deepest sea.
How my sin, tho' red like crimson, Can be whiter than the snow.
On His strength divine relying, He is all in all to me.
And forever and forever Praise and glorify the King.

REFRAIN

All that thrills my soul is Jesus; He is more than life to me; (to me;)

And the fairest of ten thousand, In my blessed Lord I see.

271 Who is He, in yonder stall

7 7. and refrain

B.R. Hanby (1833-67)

1 Who is He, in yonder stall,
At whose feet the shepherds fall?

'Tis the Lord! O wondrous story!
'Tis the Lord, the King of Glory!
At His feet we humbly fall;
Crown Him, crown Him Lord of all.

2 Who is He, in yonder cot,
Bending to His toilsome lot?

3 Who is He, in deep distress,
Fasting in the wilderness?

4 Who is He that stands and weeps
At the grave where Lazarus sleeps?

5 Lo, at midnight, who is He
Prays in dark Gethsemane?

6 Who is He, in Calvary's throes,
Asks for blessings on His foes?

7 Who is He that from the grave
Comes to heal and help and save?

8 Who is He that from His throne
Rules through all the worlds alone?

Benjamin Russell Hanby, 1833-67

419

272 Who is like unto Thee

Alternative guitar chords
for use without piano part,
in brackets.

popular version of original by
Judy Horner Montemayor
arr. Roland Fudge

Who— is like un-to thee,_____ O—
Lord a-mong gods?_____ Who— is like un-to thee_____
glor-ious in Ho-li-ness_____ fear-ful in
prai-ses_____ do-ing won-ders_____
who— is like un-to thee._____

273 Within the veil

Quiet and gentle

Ruth Dryden

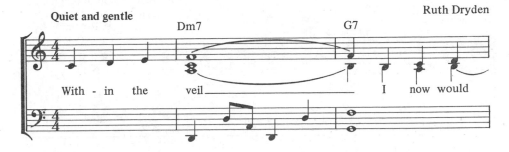

With - in the veil_____ I now would

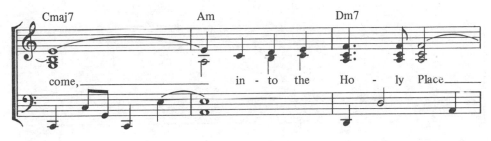

come,_____ in - to the Ho - ly Place____

___ to look up - on Thy face.____ I see such beau - ty there____

___ no oth - er can com - pare,____ I wor - ship

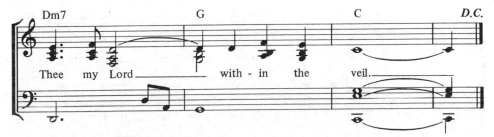

Thee my Lord____ with - in the veil.

274   Who is on the Lord's side?

ARMAGEDDON 65.65.D with Refrain

Adapted by J. Goss (1800-80)

1 Who is on the Lord's side?
    Who will serve the King?
Who will be His helpers
    Other lives to bring?
Who will leave the world's side?
    Who will face the foe?
Who is on the Lord's side?
    Who for Him will go?
        By Thy call of mercy,
            By Thy grace divine,
        We are on the Lord's side;
            Saviour, we are Thine.

2 Not for weight of glory,
    Not for crown or palm,
Enter we the army,
    Raise the warrior-psalm,
But for love that claimeth
    Lives for whom He died:
He whom Jesus nameth
    Must be on His side.
        By Thy love constraining,
            By Thy grace divine,
        We are on the Lord's side;
            Saviour, we are Thine.

3 Fierce may be the conflict,
    Strong may be the foe,
But the King's own army
    None can overthrow.
Round His standard ranging,
    Victory is secure,
For His truth unchanging
    Makes the triumph sure.
        Joyfully enlisting,
            By Thy grace divine,
        We are on the Lord's side;
            Saviour, we are Thine.

4 Chosen to be soldiers
    In an alien land,
Chosen, called, and faithful,
    For our captain's band,
In the service royal
    Let us not grow cold;
Let us be right loyal,
    Noble, true and bold.
        Master, Thou wilt keep us,
            By Thy grace divine,
        Always on the Lord's side,
            Saviour, always Thine.

Frances Ridley Havergal, 1836-79

275 Will your anchor hold

W.J. Kirkpatrick (1838-1921)

1 Will your anchor hold in the storms of life,
  When the clouds unfold their wings of strife?
  When the strong tides lift, and the cables strain,
  Will your anchor drift, or firm remain?
    We have an anchor that keeps the soul
    Steadfast and sure while the billows roll;
    Fastened to the rock which cannot move,
    Grounded firm and deep in the Saviour's love!

2 Will your anchor hold in the straits of fear?
  When the breakers roar and the reef is near;
  While the surges rage, and the wild winds blow,
  Shall the angry waves then your bark o'erflow?
    We have an anchor. . . .

3 Will your anchor hold in the floods of death,
  When the waters cold chill your latest breath?
  On the rising tide you can never fail,
  While your anchor holds within the veil.
    We have an anchor. . . .

4 Will your eyes behold through the morning light
  The city of gold and the harbour bright?
  Will you anchor safe by the heavenly shore,
  When life's storms are past for evermore?
    We have an anchor. . . .

                    Priscilla Jane Owens, 1829-99

276 Worthy art Thou O Lord

D. Richards

Thoughtfully

Wor-thy art Thou O Lord our God of ho-nour and power,

For You are reign-ing now on high, Hal-le-lu-

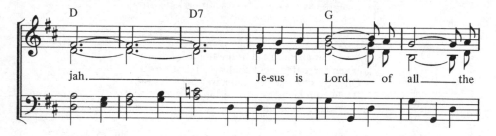

jah. Je-sus is Lord of all the

earth, Hal-le-lu- jah, Hal-le-lu-

jah, Hal-le-lu- jah.

277 Yesterday, today, for ever

Capo 1

Yes-ter-day, to-day, for ev-er, Je-sus is the same; ___

All may change, but Je-sus nev-er, Glo-ry to His Name! ___

glo-ry to His Name! ___ glo-ry to His Name! ___

All may change, but Je-sus nev-er, Glo-ry to His Name! ___

278 Ye servants of God

LAUDATE DOMINUM 55.55.65.65

C.H.H. Parry (1848-1918)

Capo 3

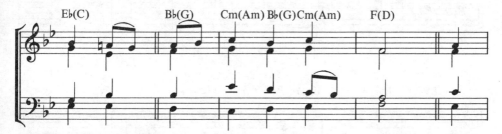

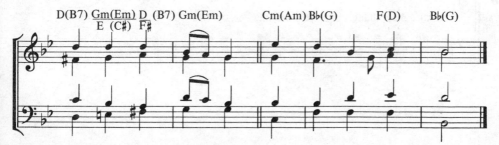

1 Ye servants of God,
    Your Master proclaim,
And publish abroad
    His wonderful name;
The name all-victorious
    Of Jesus extol;
His kingdom is glorious,
    And rules over all.

2 God ruleth on high,
    Almighty to save;
And still He is nigh,
    His presence we have;
The great congregation
    His triumph shall sing,
Ascribing salvation
    To Jesus our King.

3 "Salvation to God
    Who sits on the throne",
Let all cry aloud,
    And honour the Son;
The praises of Jesus
    The angels proclaim,
Fall down on their faces,
    And worship the Lamb.

4 Then let us adore,
    And give Him His right –
All glory and power,
    All wisdom and might;
All honour and blessing,
    With angels above;
And thanks never-ceasing,
    And infinite love.

Charles Wesley 1707-88 , altd.

279 You are the King of Glory

Words and Music M. Ford

With majesty

You are the King of Glo-ry, You are the Prince of Peace,
You are the Lord of heav'n and earth, You're the Son of right-eous-ness.
An-gels bow down be-fore_ You, Wor-ship and a-dore, for
You have the words of e-ter-nal life,_ You are Je-sus Christ the Lord._ Ho-
san-na to the Son of Da-vid!_ Ho-san-na to the King of_ kings!

Glo-ry in the high-est hea - ven, for Je-sus the Mess-i-ah reigns.

280 Worthy is the Lamb

Arr. Roland Fudge

Slow

1 Worthy is the Lamb
Worthy is the Lamb
Worthy is the Lamb
Worthy is the Lamb.

2 Holy is the Lamb
Holy is the Lamb
Holy is the Lamb
Holy is the Lamb.

3 Precious is the Lamb
Precious is the Lamb
Precious is the Lamb
Precious is the Lamb.

4 Praises to the Lamb
Praises to the Lamb
Praises to the Lamb
Praises to the Lamb

5 Glory to the Lamb
Glory to the Lamb
Glory to the Lamb
Glory to the Lamb.

6 Jesus is our Lamb
Jesus is our Lamb
Jesus is our Lamb
Jesus is our Lamb.

281 You shall go out with joy

S. Dauermann
arr. Roland Fudge

You shall go out with joy— and be led forth with peace,— and the
mount-ains and the hills shall break forth be-fore you. There'll be
shouts of joy— and the trees of the field shall—
clap, shall clap their hands and the

TREES OF THE FIELD

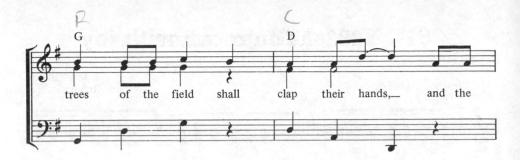

trees of the field shall clap their hands,__ and the

trees of the field shall clap their hands__ and the

trees of the field shall clap their hands__ and

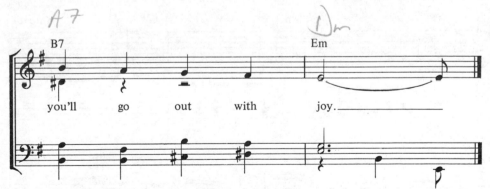

you'll go out with joy._____

282   You're alive

G. Kendrick

* The word "Alleluia" can be sung antiphonally, as indicated, the people having been divided into three equal groups.

† Final repeat of chorus is optional.

1 Led like a lamb
 To the slaughter
 In silence and shame
 There on your back
 You carried a world
 Of violence and pain
 Bleeding, dying
 Bleeding, dying.

 You're alive
 You're alive
 You have risen!
 Alleluia
 And the power
 And the glory
 Is given
 Alleluia
 Jesus to you.

2 At break of dawn
 Poor Mary
 Still weeping she came
 When through her grief
 She heard your voice
 Now speaking her name
 Mary, Master
 Mary, Master.

 You're alive. . . .

3 At the right hand
 Of the Father
 Now seated on high
 You have begun
 Your eternal reign
 Of justice and joy
 Glory, glory
 Glory, glory.

 You're alive. . . . (Repeat as required)

Using the Chord Chart

This chart contains all the chords you will need to play all the hymns and songs in this book. Even if a chord looks more difficult than those you are used to playing, DO TRY. Always seek to improve your knowledge and playing ability. It may seem to you that you have a very large number of chords to learn, but don't panic! For example, look at Fm, F# m, Gm and G# m, and you will see that they all have the same finger formation, but are on different frets for each chord. So, if you learn the ONE finger formation, you can immediately play *four new chords!*

If you want to play chords in a different key to the one set (because, for example, of a limited chord knowledge) you can very simply use this chart to discover the chords you need. Here's how you do it:

1. Locate the key chord that is set in the original. Find it on the chart in the SECOND COLUMN for *major* keys and the THIRD COLUMN for *minor* keys.
2. Locate on the chart the new key that you wish to play the music in (also in the second column for *major* keys and the third column for *minor* keys).
3. Work out the rest of the chords that need to be changed by noting their position around the original key chord and finding the chord that is *in exactly the same position* around the new key chord.

Example:
When changing from key chord F to key chord E, find F and E in the second column of the chart. On the left of F you will find C7. The equivalent chord in key E is therefore the one on the left of E, B7. Similarly Dm would become C# m, and B♭ would become A.

Chord Chart

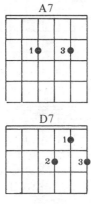
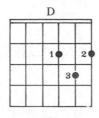
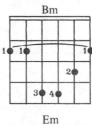
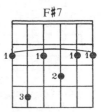

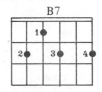

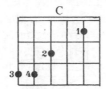

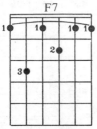

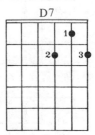

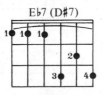
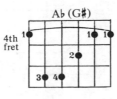

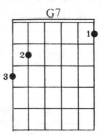

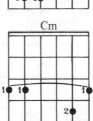

Ab7 (G#7)
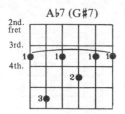

2nd. fret
3rd.
4th.

Db (C#)
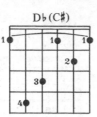

Bbm (A#m)
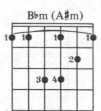

F7
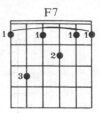

C#7 (Db7)
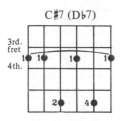

3rd. fret
4th.

F# (Gb)
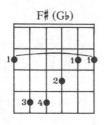

D#m (Ebm)
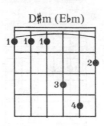

A#7 (Bb7)
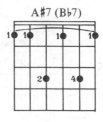

F#7 (Gb7)
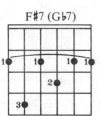

B
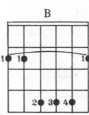

G#m (Abm)
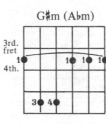

3rd. fret
4th.

D#7 (Eb7)
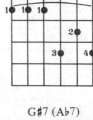

B7
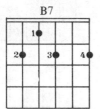

E
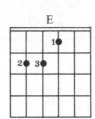

C#m (Dbm)
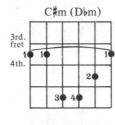

3rd. fret
4th.

G#7 (Ab7)
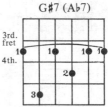

3rd. fret
4th.

E7
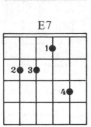

A
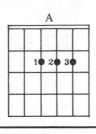

F#m (Gbm)
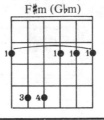

C#7 (Db7)
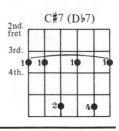

2nd. fret
3rd.
4th.

Ddim or G#(Ab)dim

Adim, D#dim, Ebdim, F#dim, Gbdim, Cdim

Edim, Gdim, A#dim, Bbdim, C#dim, Dbdim
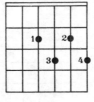

Fdim, Bdim
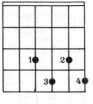

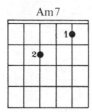
Am7

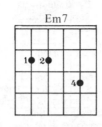
Bbm7

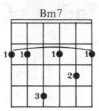
Bm7

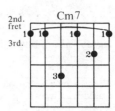
Cm7

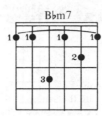

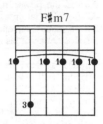

Dm7 · Em7 · Fm7 · F#m7

Gm7 · Asus4 · A7sus4 · B7sus4

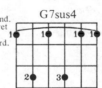

Csus4 · Dsus4 · D7sus4 · Esus4

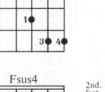

E7sus4 · Fsus4 · G7sus4 · Cmaj7

Dmaj7 · Fmaj7 · Gmaj7 · Amaj7

C6 · D6 · G6 · Am6

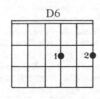
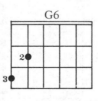

Index of First Lines

Titles in italics, where different from the first line.

Alternative words for verses 2 and 3 of Song 21

2 God has many gifts
  Given by his Son —
  Building the Body of Christ
  Creating a faith that is one;
    Bind us together. . . .

3 We are the family of God,
  Joined by the Spirit above,
  Working together with Christ
  Growing and building in love:
    Bind us together. . . .

Biblical and Thematic Index

(C = Chorus)

1. INDEX OF BIBLICAL REFERENCES

		Song No.			Song No.			Song No.
Matt.	18.20	C13, 68, 233	Rom.	5.5	34	Col.	1.16	192
	25.4	58		5.8	57		1.18	217
Mark	5.27	C193		5.11	168		3.15–16	157, 184
	14.36	C1		6.13	104		3.23	55
Luke	1.46	159, 215		8.13	C127			
	2.7	271		8.15	C1	1 Thes.	5.17	214
	3.16	174		10.15	79			
	4.18	64		12.1	212	1 Tim.	1.7	103
	15.4	35		13.11	169		6.12	49
	15.6	10, 101		16.26	269			
	23.33	230				2 Tim.	1.12	89, 100
	24.29	2	1 Cor.	1.18	258		3.15	177
	24.36	125		1.23	139			
				1.24	17	Heb.	2.9	220
John	1.11	237		3.15	76		4.7	169
	1.14	120		10.4	197		6.19	C273, 275
	1.29	132		15.22	191		12.1	51, 157
	3.5	223		15.52	268		12.2	158, 249
	3.7	245		15.57	238			
	3.16	223		16.13	211	Jas.	1.17	62
	4.14	38, 59, 85					2.19	126
	5	168	2 Cor.	3.18	149			
	6.35	63, 80		10.5	152	1 Pet.	2.5	27
	6.48	128		12.9	82		2.7	78
	6.68	279					2.9	C31, 206
	8.36	245	Gal.	2.20	101, 160		2.24	258
	9.25	168, 143		6.14	107, 256		3.12	262
	10.11	243					5.5	34
	11.25	80	Eph.	1.7	8			
	12.26	172		2.1	143	1 John	4.14	83
	12.32	139		2.7	78		4.16	106
	14.1–6	42		2.8	10		4.19	110
	15.4	2		2.20	27, 217			
	15.10	106		3.19	25, 112	Rev.	1.5	248
	15.14	262		4.1	152		1.7	141
	16.8	89		4.5	217, 247		1.18	150
	19.34	197		5.9	36		4.1	33
	20.11	282		5.25	217		4.8	73
	20.22	25, 164, 170		6.10ff	207		4.11	242
				6.18	190, 214		5.12	37, 280
	20.25	70, 146					6.2	5, 238
	21.15	116	Phil.	1.6	180		7.10	278
				2.5	157		11.15	123
Acts	2.3	34		2.7	11, 57		14.1	39, 278
	3.6	C199		2.9	232		19.1	67
	3.8	168		2.10	15, C69, 236		19.6	C65
	4.12	230		3.8	258		19.12	39
	16.26	11, 123, 143		3.9	162		19.16	C3
				4.4	C194, 195		21.2	27
							21.4	158, 208
							22.1	270

2. INDEX OF THEMES